A TYPICAL EXTRAORDINARY JEW

From Tarnow to Jerusalem

Calvin Goldscheider
and
Jeffrey M. Green

Hamilton Books
A member of
The Rowman & Littlefield Publishing Group
Lanham · Boulder · New York · Toronto · Plymouth, UK

Copyright © 2011 by
Hamilton Books
4501 Forbes Boulevard
Suite 200
Lanham, Maryland 20706
Hamilton Books Acquisitions Department (301) 459-3366

Estover Road
Plymouth PL6 7PY
United Kingdom

Library of Congress Control Number: 2011931913
ISBN: 978-0-7618-5643-6 (paperback : alk. paper)
eISBN: 978-0-7618-5644-3

Permission for cover photo granted by
Yad Vashem The Holocaust Martyrs' and Heroes' Remembrance Authority,
Jerusalem, Israel.

To the memory of

Shmuel and Esther Braw

and

in honor of their children

Rivka and Mal

Contents

Introducing Shmuel   vii

Chapter 1:   A Personal Pilgrimage to Tarnow,
                 Poland, 2008   1

Chapter 2:   "It Happened, but It Didn't Happen"   11

Chapter 3:   "A City in My Bones"   21

Chapter 4:   "A Shtinkindike Shtik Flaish"   35

Chapter 5:   "How Far will it Go"   53

Chapter 6:   "I Wasn't Lucky in Australia"   71

Chapter 7:   "They Dry Out"   87

Chapter 8:   "Not Lonely but Lost"   99

Chapter 9:   "A Normal Life"   109

Chapter 10:   New Places   117

Chapter 11:   A Poem about Tarnow   121

Epilogue: Kibbutz Ein Zurim, Israel, July 2008   135

Introducing Shmuel

"I am not a man of hatred. What I want after the war, I didn't get till now. That after the experience, the suffering, that it would make them different people. But they haven't changed. They're worse. They learned how to kill more, to suffer more, how to punish people more. I'm disappointed. I'm very disappointed in people in general. I wanted people to be kind to each other after the war."

Shmuel Braw forced himself on us with his magnetic personality and dramatic stories about his life. We did not interview him because we wanted to write another book about a Holocaust survivor. We interviewed him because his conversation and his stories were so engaging that he barely left us with any choice. Now we are finally writing the book—his book.

Calvin originally met Shmuel Braw at a synagogue in Jerusalem:

In the early 1970s after I had immigrated to Israel with my family and purchased a home in Talpiot, a southern suburb of Jerusalem, I began to attend the local synagogue there. It was a grand, somewhat cavernous structure, a former warehouse that had been converted into a place of worship and named after the world famous writer, a local resident, and Nobel Prize winner, Shmuel Yosef Agnon. The spectacular, carved wooden ark had been retrieved from a small town in Italy and restored to its former luster. I purchased two seats there, one for me and one for my son Judah. We sat in the second row, on the right side of the central *bima* where the reader would lead the congregation in prayer. In front of me sat Harold Schimmel, the poet and translator. And at the other end of my row was a vigorous, retired gentleman, small in stature, who appeared friendly and kind and who regularly greeted me warmly on the Sabbath. He was part of a small group of retired men who found temporary rental housing

subsidized by the Israeli government in this corner of Jerusalem. Every once in a
while he would take his turn leading the prayers. His voice was sweet and
gentle. He obviously knew the prayers well. His accent was not the Sephardic
Israeli accent of a native Israeli but was a well-practiced Ashkenazic Hebrew.
His suit, shirt and tie were modest but neat and revealed his European origins.
He was a short, spry man who loved hearing music and singing. His accent in
English was a unique blend of Australian, Yiddish, and Polish.

Every once in a while he would engage me and my son in some conversation about Israel or about my teaching or research at the Hebrew University
in Jerusalem or about my son Judah's school. I inquired about his health and his
post-retirement activities. He always seemed to be busy, painting someone's
apartment, helping out a friend, visiting with some relatives in Jerusalem or
elsewhere, or dealing with the Israeli bureaucracy.

On Friday evenings the Rabbi of the synagogue would give a short dis-
course on the weekly Torah portion. While I very much liked the Rabbi and
sometimes found his weekly talks of interest, I generally used the fifteen
minutes or so to study the weekly Torah portion or a Mishnah text on my own.
However, Shmuel Braw often came between me and my studies by chatting with
me or my son. His spoken Hebrew was not extensive, and he didn't even try to
understand the Rabbi's talk. He was knowledgeable but not a scholar. One Friday night, while the Rabbi was speaking, Shmuel leaned over and whispered
that he had had a dream the night before, actually a nightmare. He then said in a
low voice "but now is not the time to tell you about it." I was captivated! On the
way home from services that Friday night he began to tell me tantalizing stories
about his life, half in Yiddish and half in Australian accented English.

He said he went to bed quite late to be certain of sleeping until the next
morning. Sometimes nightmares woke him and then he knew he wouldn't get
back to sleep. Though he had mentioned his nightmares to attract my attention,
he never actually told me about their content. However, having learned that he
lost his wife, their only daughter, his mother, two sisters, their husbands and
children and countless other relatives and friends during the Second World War,
and that he himself was a survivor of a Siberian labor camp, I could easily
imagine what his bad dreams were about.

I listened to his stories, and the more I heard, the more I wanted to learn
about his life, which had included many of the most dramatic, painful, and

joyful events of European Jews in the twentieth century. I decided to try and record these stories and piece them together into a coherent narrative. I invited Shmuel to spend several evenings with me and talk about what he had lived through. The idea appealed to him. Perhaps he had been wondering how long it would take me to come up with the idea.

I asked Jeff Green, a friend from the neighborhood who also attended the synagogue, to meet with Shmuel and me to help me record the details of Shmuel's life, because I thought the literary and human aspect of the project would interest him. We met usually once a week, over a long period of time. Jeff and I conferred before each session and prepared for the evening session by carefully outlining some of the themes that we wanted to learn from Shmuel's life. We were rarely successful in keeping the conversation on track. Shmuel was also preparing for these sessions, and he too had a set of topics that he wanted to convey to us. We became a team—a social scientist, a writer, and Shmuel—and that created its own dynamic.

In one of the early sessions we said that we would concentrate on the early years from when Shmuel was born in 1906 in Tarnow, in what would later be Poland, until he went to work in Berlin for his brother-in-law, in 1929. "That's twenty-three years," he reminded us! How could we have the temerity to think that we could find out about such a period of time in a couple of hours? In my study, where we met with him, the walls were lined with books. He would look all around and said with some satisfaction pointing to himself, "You have here a living book." He was right of course. On another occasion when we had moved on to the war period and proposed to spend our session on the period from 1939 to 1945, Shmuel said: "If I told you day by day what happened to me in those six years you could fill up three of your books" pointing to one of the shelves in my study.

When we first began to interview Shmuel formally, my goal, as a social scientist, was to put a human face on the broader picture of Jewish trans-formation in Europe that I had written about over several years before I met Shmuel. I wanted to illustrate the themes of change and continuity among Jewish communities with qualitative insights from diverse persons of European origin living in Jerusalem. I planned not only on interviewing Shmuel but also his neighbor from Romania who had escaped to France during the war, his friend from Hungary who ended up in New York, his synagogue seat-mate who hid in the forests of Lithuania during the war with the help of Christian school friends. Over time I had also wanted to interview their wives who I was sure had different experiences and perceptions of their families and their European experiences. They all came from somewhat different places in Central and Eastern Europe, they all had survived the war years, moved on to new lives in diverse places, and then after many years came to share a neighborhood in Jerusalem. They had many things in common, despite very different origins and experiences. Their shared language was Yiddish and they now shared Jerusalem and living in Israel.

I never managed to carry out my broader project of learning how each one of these persons had a rich history to share because we fell under Shmuel's spell – which suited Jeff's more literary goal of coming to understand a single, fascinating individual. In fact, Jeff and I didn't manage even to carry out our smaller project of writing a book based on Shmuel's stories, mainly because I became deeply attached to Shmuel and his family. I am a social scientist, and the books that I write are based on research, statistics, and sociological and demographical theories. To write about a man whom I had come to love simply didn't fit into my self-image as an objective scholar.

Jeff adds:

My role in this project was tertiary. The primary role was Shmuel's. Though I was never as close to him as Calvin was, I also found him utterly enchanting. Calvin's close friendship with Shmuel is the main channel of the project, but Shmuel enjoyed having an audience, and my presence doubled its size. Calvin brought extensive Jewish knowledge to the project as well as the perspective of his profession—the sociological and historical understanding of the processes of modernization as they affected the Jews of Eastern Europe. I brought curiosity, empathy, and appreciation of Shmuel's literary skill as a storyteller. After we interviewed Shmuel, I was the one who transcribed the tapes and organized the material in preliminary fashion.

I had come to Israel with my wife and our eldest daughter in 1973 with a doctorate in Comparative Literature from Harvard and extensive familiarity with the Renaissance in France but not too much knowledge about Judaism or Jewish history. By the time Calvin approached me and asked me to participate in this project, I had realized that I was no longer interested in pursuing an academic career, and I wasn't sure what I wanted to do or could do. I was seeking an authentic way of being Jewish, and getting to know Shmuel and hearing his stories gave me important insight into what that might mean.

The bulk of these interviews took place in the mid-1970s. Unfortunately, the equipment we used to record the interviews was worse than rudimentary, and we didn't save the barely audible tapes. The time that has passed since we interviewed him has made Shmuel's stories even more precious and the loss of the sound of his voice even more regrettable. By now, anyone who lived through the years before World War II as an adult would be about a hundred years old. There is almost no one left who can tell stories like these.

We considered trying to publish a book based on them at the time, giving Shmuel another name to preserve his privacy, but the results were unsatisfactory to us, and we set the project aside. Calvin moved back to the United States and on to a distinguished career as a professor at Brown, and I became a free-lance translator and sometime writer. Calvin and I remained friends, and when he contacted me, after his pilgrimage to Tarnow, telling me that he wanted to revise and expand the rough draft we had prepared, I was delighted. I had not looked at the material or thought about it very much for twenty years or more, and when I reread it, I was overwhelmed by its richness, and of course by my personal memories of Shmuel.

Calvin concludes:

What Jeff and I learned from Shmuel's story of surviving and his construction of the life before and after the destruction of European Jewry was both deeply personal and singularly illustrative. Shmuel's attitudes and experiences in pre-war Poland were a lesson about the sources of Jewish values, about the living Jewish tradition, about families, about Jewish history and about how we should think about Jewish futures. He taught us about much more than survival in the hell that was the European Holocaust.

A decade and a half after Shmuel's death in 1992, I made a trip to Tarnow, Shmuel's hometown in Poland, with my wife, Fran, Shmuel's daughter Rivka, and a research colleague from Sweden, originally from Poland. That trip, in honor of Shmuel's memory, triggered a decision to reread and revise the

material that Jeff and I had collected from Shmuel. To publish it now is further
tribute to the memory of that typical extraordinary Jew.

Chapter One

A Personal Pilgrimage to Tarnow Poland, 2008

The train from Krakow to Tarnow takes the visitor through eighty kilometers of small towns and farms, some factories, and forests with dense green trees. It took about an hour. Four of us shared a compartment: my wife Fran and I, American professors of sociology, Rivka Jaffi, an Israeli woman whose late father was born in Tarnow, and Danuta Biterman, a colleague and friend from Stockholm, Sweden who was born and raised in Warsaw.

Each of us was lost in quiet thought, anticipating the excitement of exploring together a city to which we felt a strong personal attachment, though none of us had ever been there. Rivka and I had heard a lot about it from Rivka's father, Shmuel Braw, who had died over a dozen years before—and he had not been in Tarnow, the city of his birth, since he left it in 1945. Fran and Danuta knew about Shmuel's Tarnow from what I had told them about him and his town.

The four of us had met in Krakow a day earlier, after months of planning. Fran and I came from our home in Washington, DC; Rivka came from Tel Aviv, Israel; and Danuta came from her current home in Sweden. We prepared ourselves by reading history books and Internet reports, but most importantly by recalling Shmuel Braw, a man I had come to love almost as a second father. He had told Rivka and me stories about growing up in Tarnow, about the three times he returned there: from Budapest after World War I, from Berlin after his father fell ill in the early 1930s, and from Siberia after World War II. Through him, we were connected with his family and the Jewish community there, the people of Tarnow whom he loved and who loved him—his friends, his family, his neighbors, and the city itself. He spoke of his first wife Frieda, their home in

Tarnow, and their daughter Esther. Though he lived in other places—Italy, Australia, and Israel—Tarnow remained the most important place in his life.

He told me about his return to Tarnow from Siberia after the war, to a Tarnow that was no longer his, and about his final departure. During the two decades of our friendship, I had regularly asked him to go back to Tarnow and show his town to me. I wanted to share through his eyes the Tarnow that was and is no more. At first he said no, he would never go back. It would be too painful to see the reality. He had beautiful and vivid memories of his Tarnow, his home and his people and he wanted to retain these images of the past. But, as always, I pressed. On a final visit to his kibbutz home in Ein Zurim, Israel where he lived with his second wife Esther and his daughter Rivka and her family, the last time I saw him, he was depressed, his heart was weak and he was confused. He was dying. He was no longer the robust, smiling, and energetic Shmuel I had grown to love. He was a shadow of his former self, shuffling rather than walking, deteriorating in body and soul. Finally, and I knew reluctantly, he agreed to go to Tarnow with me, his "Colvin." But when he did agree, we both knew it was too late. He was just trying to please me—the "professor," whom he loved, maybe as the son he never had. He passed away several months later in his home in Ein Zurim, with Rivka and Esther by his side. He had moved with Esther from Jerusalem, where I first met him and grew fond of him, to Ein Zurim to be with his daughter Rivka and her family. He thought that Esther would be more comfortable in the kibbutz closer to family after she was widowed (since Shmuel was several years older than Esther and in poorer health). Shmuel was always planning ahead, thinking about others, and particularly about his family.

Our visit to Tarnow was in honor of Shmuel's memory. He had made us curious about the place, and we wondered what we would find there in 2008. Would we be able to feel what Shmuel loved about his city? Would we find the remnants of his family? His home? His friends and their offspring? Would we find the cemetery where his family was buried? Would we locate some Jewish community that was functioning if not thriving? In 1939 there were about 25,000 Jews living in Tarnow, about half the total population. During the war years Jews from the surrounding villages and towns were gathered into ghettos in Tarnow, increasing the Jewish population by another 15,000. We knew their fate. All fled or were killed; a very few like Shmuel returned briefly after the war only to leave for new places. Had any Jews remained of the Zionists,

Bundists, the secular and the Hasidim? Were there remnants of Jewish institutions—synagogues, cultural centers, political and social organizations, ritual baths, cemeteries? Could we at least find the businesses and homes that had been owned by Jews? We knew to expect little if anything but we didn't have a "feeling" (as Shmuel often said) for what that meant until we were actually there.

Early in the morning before the summer sun was at its peak we entered Tarnow through the railroad station, an edifice in neo-classical style, probably dating back to the Habsburg Monarchy, impressive in its size and height, with huge columns, and undergoing refurbishment. A friend or cousin of Danuta's from Warsaw put us in contact with Arek, a resident of Tarnow, who offered to help us explore the city and learn its history. Arek was Polish-born a man in his mid-30s, short, round face and closely cropped hair, with a pale complexion, not particularly distinctive among the residents of Tarnow. He turned out to be a high school history teacher in Tarnow, married, the father of one son. Born and raised in Tarnow, he had made himself an expert on contemporary Polish history and knowledgeable about the Jews of Tarnow, particularly of the Holocaust. He had been to Israel, visited Yad Vashem, gathering information there for his high school students. He was eager to share his knowledge of the Tarnow Jewish community that was and the effects of the Holocaust on the Jews and on his town. He spoke almost no English but he had much to say in Polish, which Danuta translated for us. We could not have found a better guide to contemporary Tarnow and its Jewish history. We assumed he was Jewish, and it was not until the end of our day with him that we discovered he was not.

Tarnow is a town like hundreds of others in Poland and elsewhere in Europe. There are shops and restaurants, some old and some new. When we arrived, we found the streets busy and the atmosphere quite lively. Some of the buildings are hundreds of years old, including the town hall, now a museum in the center of town, a Gothic Cathedral originally built in the fourteenth century, and remnants of the seventeenth century city wall. We saw tourist shops and churches in the narrow streets of the town center, as well as new department stores and movie theaters.

Before the Second World War, Jews had been heavily concentrated in the city, comprising the fourth largest Jewish population center in Galicia, where they were a distinctive social minority, marked by where they lived and prayed, by where they went to school, and by their distinctive occupations. Some but certainly not all wore clothing (long black coats and fur hats) that separated them from their non-Jewish friends and neighbors. Most of the younger generation in the 1920s and 1930s had shed the traditional Hasidic garb of their fathers, built new and more decorous synagogues, often went to public schools, and spoke fluent Polish. They were clearly Jewish but had entered a new world of opportunity and independence, less constrained by the traditions of their elders and open to the changes taking place in their community.

The Jewish Tarnow of the pre-World War II era is mostly gone, eliminated, destroyed with only a few visible reminders of what was—a Jewish star in concrete on some building, a plaque on another, an inscription in Yiddish that still advertises a restaurant menu, and empty indentations on doorposts where the ritual parchment of the Mezuzah had been inserted. Some Hebrew writing can be found here and there if you look for it; Jewish residential areas of the past are mainly empty lots, overgrown by weeds and years of neglect or replaced by buildings and flats constructed by the Communist government in places that were first destroyed by the Nazis. Between the destruction of the two regimes almost nothing Jewish remains.

One exception are the columns and pillars of the old synagogue rising thirty or so feet above a large, abandoned field close to the middle of town. The majesty of the synagogue can only be imagined and reconstructed from the pictures that are available. The columns are stark and impressive—and lonely, a reminder that not everything can be destroyed. There is a plaque noting that the Nazis burned down the synagogue. The surrounding area is no longer Jewish in any way. Not far away is the former *mikvah*, the Jewish public ritual bath. It is still a beautiful building in Moorish style suggesting the grandeur of the past, but it now houses a restaurant. Across from the former *mikvah* is a monument to those (Poles) who were sent to Auschwitz in 1940. Jews are not mentioned on the description of the monument. Over 3,000 Jews were killed in the market place in Tarnow in June 1942 and other Jews were herded into the *mikvah* building before being shipped to Auschwitz.

On our way out of the starkness of the former Jewish quarter, we passed by an open area that had been the meeting place frequented by a number of Jewish organizations: socialists, Zionists, Bundists and Agudah organizations, which tried to mobilize Jews in the interwar period to protest against their treatment by the Poles and the Germans. We would not have known that by what we saw except for the testimony of Arek, our guide. The Talmud Torah, Jewish community library, and orphanage now house local Polish institutions.

On the outskirts of the city proper is a large locked Jewish cemetery, fenced in on all sides. Arek obtained the key and led us through the gate. It was a hot summer day, and we were the only visitors. Most of the several thousand graves were of Jews who died before the war. In the first area beyond the locked gate of the cemetery were the graves of Rabbis, the elite of the Jewish community, Kohanim (priests), and orphans and young children. The graves of women were in the back of the cemetery, since families were separated by gender in this cemetery as in many others. The graves are packed together, several thousands from the pre-World War II period, neglected, names missing or faded by the ravages of time, broken stones turned over. The graves were overgrown by weeds and the cemetery itself was populated by scurrying cats. It was eerie to walk around the cemetery, hoping to see something of the beauty and history of Jewish Tarnow.

Rivka and I wandered about for quite a while in search for the graves of Shmuel's family. We had a photograph of the graves but no indication of where they were. We stopped our search after a while. It was somehow fitting that we failed to find monuments or gravestones for the last remnants of Shmuel's family. Arek's version of the Holocaust time period in Tarnow was meticulous and balanced historically. But, perhaps because of his orientation as a history teacher and the need to translate his Polish, his review appeared cold and impersonal to us. The overwhelming sadness that we felt in the cemetery contrasted powerfully with his careful objectivity.

The cemetery was overgrown and neglected, a poor indication of the lively community where Jews had lived before the War. It was like a black and white film in contrast to the colorful city that we had just seen. Even in the heat of summer, there was an overall atmosphere of dead grayness.

A tall monument stands about fifty feet from the entrance to the cemetery, a memorial to the Jews from Tarnow who were killed in the Holocaust. We stood before it and I recited "*El Moleh Rahamin*" (God, full of mercy), the memorial prayer, from Rivka's tattered prayer book. I needed Fran's and Rivka's help to complete the prayer. I choked up and could barely say the Kaddish. My tears and emotions overcame me. I lost no family in Tarnow; it was not the city of my ancestors. My only personal connection to Tarnow was through Shmuel and his stories. For me, as for Fran and Danuta, the cemetery, grave stones, and monument were the final resting places for "every Jew" of every town and city in Poland, millions, young and old, nameless but not forgotten. For Rivka, it was where her actual ancestors were buried, and for her sake we regretted that we couldn't find the Braw family graves, Shmuel's father and mother, his relatives and friends. Would they be remembered in another generation except through another of Arek's history lessons?

Symbolically and ritually, we all washed our hands behind the building in the corner of the cemetery where the shrouded bodies had been prepared for burial. Arek returned my spare *kippah*, which he had borrowed to cover his head, since even as a non-Jew he felt that the Jewish cemetery, like a synagogue, was a sacred place. We parted for the old railway station on our way back to Krakow, passing signs in the station for the next train stop—Auschwitz. In the heat of a summer's day I shivered in pain at the thought of that place.

The Jews of Tarnow had a rich history, which we had come to know because of our connection to Shmuel and his memories. Tarnow had famous Rabbis and teachers, Jewish leaders and well known families, religious institutions, schools, and clubs, welfare and political organizations, ritual slaughter houses and ritual baths. Today Tarnow has no Jewish community or future. There are only the Jewish dead in the cemetery and occasional visitors— no Jewish children, no institutions, no marking of holidays, no public or private displays of Judaism. We visited the city on the first day of the Hebrew month of Tammuz, a special joyous day like the beginning of every Jewish lunar month. It felt like Tisha B'Av to me, the ninth day of the month of Av, marking the destruction of the Temples in Jerusalem and the exile of Jews from their homes.

We cried not only because of the Holocaust and the unfathomable numbers of Jews murdered in Tarnow as in hundreds of places throughout Europe. We cried for the end of the Jewish community in Tarnow. The end of Jewish history in Tarnow. We cried for Shmuel and his family. Shmuel surely ran about these streets as a child, walked through them as a young man, and saw some of the buildings that we saw. He had a home there, and a business, and employees, and friends and family. All these were gone, without a trace except in his mind and now in ours.

Rivka visualized "Shmilik" (as she affectionately referred to her father) here and there in the streets of Tarnow. She took photographs as we walked the streets, repeating: "He must have seen that building"; "he must have run in this narrow alley"; "maybe Shmilik walked this street" in the old quarter of the city; was this the station where he boarded trains on his way to see family and friends in Berlin and Krakow? Rivka tried to capture what was in her father's vision as he grew up in Tarnow, planning to share these scenes with her mom and her family. Shmuel had lived the first half of his life in Tarnow, but we couldn't see that or capture it on film. We heard him again and again in our imagination as we walked the streets. His Tarnow, the one that really interests us, is in the stories that he told to convey the inner life of Tarnow of a generation earlier.

Tarnow in 2008 is our story, and this book contains Shmuel's stories. Our story is brief; Shmuel's stories are rich and detailed and we are only partially and selectively able to reconstruct them. The two stories are not easy to disentangle. When we were in Tarnow we were looking for Shmuel—where he might have run around as a child, where he played and where he prayed; the trains that he took, the clubs he frequented, the *mikvah* he went to, the streets and buildings that he saw; his home and his business; the graves of his family members. We tried very hard to reconstruct Shmuel's Tarnow from the stories that he had told to me and to Rivka, about the life he lived there. As we searched in today's Tarnow for the place where Shmuel lived, it became clear that the Tarnow that he knew cannot be reconstructed from the physical remains. There are but faint footprints, hints of what was: buried clues. Only in our imagination can we capture what was Shmuel's Tarnow, and that imagination was colored and populated by his stories.

Our party of four returned to Krakow for Shabbat where we went to the Remah synagogue (built in the fifteenth century) for a prayer service in the morning. A guest cantor originally from Krakow chanted the prayers with just the right Galicianer tune and accent that I am certain would have pleased Shmuel. I again imagined that at some point Shmuel prayed in this small synagogue when he was visiting Krakow. We listened to part of the Krakow Annual Jewish Festival concerts in the open square on Saturday afternoon in the rain. There were thousands of people at the outdoor concert, mostly from other areas of Europe. Few Jews are left in Krakow where there was once a large Jewish population before the war (around 60,000 in 1939, one quarter of the total). There are many rebuilt Jewish institutions that are largely used as tourist sites and museums.

Before we parted from each other on Sunday, Rivka to look for her mother's devastated community in Lwow, Danuta to Warsaw, and Fran and I to Jerusalem, we reviewed our extraordinary day in Tarnow the previous week. Near our hotel was an ice cream parlor and we sat there and explored the "highlights" of our Polish adventure. We each had a different take: For Danuta, the Swede of Polish birth and origin, the town of Tarnow, where she had never been, was the highlight of her visit and contrasted with Warsaw. The highlight for Rivka was "finding" Shmuel in the streets of Tarnow and even in Krakow, where many of his stories were set. Fran's highlight was being together with Rivka and Danuta, making personal connections and working things through. Relationships were developed that are likely to last a lifetime

I was still pondering the contrast between the colorfulness of Tarnow and the faintness of the little that remained of Jewish presence in Tarnow; the beauty of Krakow and the simplicity of the fifteenth century Remah synagogue and the end of the Jewish communities in Krakow and Tarnow, except for museums and cemeteries. I had finally begun to get the "feeling" of Jewish life the way it was described by Shmuel and the enormous sadness at the end of the Jewish world in Poland.

Along with my warm memories of Shmuel, I had quite a bit of written material, the product of extensive interviews conducted with him in the mid-1970s, in collaboration with my friend Jeff Green. Neither one of us knew quite what to do with the material at the time, and in the intervening years we were both busy with many other projects. We filed away our notes along with a typed manuscript; Shmuel was stored in our memory but not forgotten. However, after my trip to Tarnow with Shmuel's daughter, I decided to read the material again and see whether it added up to more than just the personal reminiscences of a fascinating and extremely likable man, to whom I had become very attached. I am convinced that it does.

Jeff Adds:

Our working title for this project was "A Typical Extraordinary Jew," which is how I had come to see Shmuel. He was typical, and his typicality was important to us. He was a Yiddish-speaking, Eastern European Jewish man, whose life, until the Holocaust, was in many respects similar to that of hundreds of thousands of other Jewish men roughly his age, as they stepped forward into the rapidly changing modern world. Yet he was also extraordinary: the courage, resilience, resourcefulness, intelligence, and simple humanity that enabled him to survive unspeakable horrors and rebuild his life and start a new family were admirable and outstanding.

These are Shmuel's stories. Not all of them to be sure and not even a majority of them. We taped most of the ones presented here as he told them to us in Calvin's book-lined study. Then we transcribed and organized them. Others are stories that Shmuel told Calvin at other times, which are presented as he remembers them. We share them not as history and not solely as biography but as the record of a simple, extraordinary, engaging, and charming Jew whose life reflects many of the traumas and joys of the last century of Jewish history in Europe and in Israel.

We were both enchanted by Shmuel and his stories. We discussed them extensively after we heard them and after they were written, and we did as much fact-checking as we could. Some of the stories cannot be verified and some have historical details that are not likely to be fully accurate. They present facts and events as accurately as Shmuel remembered them, and they capture his spirit. Our main concern in presenting them is to do justice to his experiences and attitudes.

Both Rivka and Malvena, Shmuel's daughters, read through earlier drafts of this manuscript, made some minor changes of fact about Shmuel's family, and confirmed that these were among the stories that they heard from their father as they were growing up. Shmuel told wonderful stories that made the listener smile and cry, fascinated by the teller as well as by the stories. Shmuel's daughters encouraged us to preserve the stories of their father so that others would come to know the complex and simple Jew, Shmuel Braw, and share some Jewish history through his eyes and experiences.

Chapter Two

"It Happened, but it Didn't Happen"

Shmuel told us that he was in the Polish army three separate times. He served once between 1927 and 1929 as a recruit, again in 1939 when the government mobilized reserves at the outbreak of World War II, and a third time in 1945 when a Polish Army in Exile was created in the Soviet Union. At first, when Shmuel said he'd been in the army for two years, we thought he meant starting from 1939, but he corrected us. "What do you mean? In six weeks it was all over. No army; No Poland; Nothing." Then we leaped to the opposite conclusion. That Shmuel had been far from the actual fighting when the Nazis overran Poland. But it turned out that he had been at the front. "So you had a gun, and you fought against the Germans in 1939," we concluded. Shmuel had a story, though, so he teased us. "Yes, I had a gun but I didn't fire a shot."

On the eve of the war his reserve unit was called up, fully equipped (except for ammunition, which they were to receive at the front), and marched about for a day to shape them up a bit. By Saturday night, September 2, they were deployed in trenches at the front in Silesia, waiting for bullets. Shmuel was crouching next to an old veteran, a Sergeant Major who had served in the Austro-Hungarian army in World War I, a fixture of the Tarnow barracks ever since Shmuel could remember: "When I was a little boy he was already in the army," he told us.

At last a truck came around with bullets. The Sergeant Major started swearing like a Polish drunk. Shmuel asked what was the matter. The man said, "I like you, you're a smart guy. Just put your bullets in your rifle." Shmuel continued, "So I opened the rifle, and they wouldn't go in. We had Polish rifles and French bullets, and at the other front you got French rifles and Polish bullets. The Sergeant said, 'We lost the war,' and that was true. He was not a loony, just plain practical. Poland was sold out."

The German bombardment started at three a.m., an overwhelming barrage of bombs, artillery and machine gun bullets. The Polish soldiers lay down and waited hopelessly. A shell fell about ten yards away killing fifteen or twenty soldiers and leaving a deep crater. "In one minute the Sergeant said to me, 'Crawl into that hole.' I followed his advice. He's an old soldier. That was the first time in my life I was in a war. I was playing soldier." Shmuel crawled in the crater with the Sergeant, taking along the rifle, bayonet everything. The Sergeant said to throw the gun away. "I couldn't believe it. But he said, 'Throw it away, what do you need it for? What good does it do you?' So I put it away next to me."

"Then something happened that makes me not only shiver, but my hair is standing on end." Shmuel puts his hands up to show us. The Sergeant began pulling corpses into the crater. "I said, 'Sergeant, what are you doing?' He told me to take a few. 'You can't help it. They're dead. Cover yourself. What difference does it make if they have a few more bullets? They will protect you. And I did." Shmuel and the Sergeant lay at the bottom of a crater underneath a pile of dead soldiers until the shelling stopped around nine the following morning. Then they started running back, away from the Germans. Only about 250 soldiers survived from Shmuel's battalion. "He saved my life," Shmuel said. The Sergeant was not a Jew and not the only gentile who would save Shmuel before the end of the war.

It took them three days to get back to Tarnow. The Polish army was in a complete shambles. Thousands of soldiers were fleeing the front. Few officers were in evidence. "I will tell you something, don't laugh" Shmuel said "The young officers in the regular army, they think it's play. When they come to war they find out it's not play. Young soldiers wet their pants. That's true. They couldn't control their stomachs."

It was hot in Poland that September. Shmuel and the Sergeant arrived in Tarnow ragged and filthy, their blistered feet wrapped in the cotton bands the Polish army issued instead of socks. They followed a rumor some seventy kilometers east to the river San, where the army was said to be regrouping. But there was no one to report to there. They returned to the Tarnow garrison. A young officer laughed at them when they showed up. He was going home and advised them to do the same. He told them to burn their uniforms, and that's just what Shmuel did.

Poland had collapsed. Shmuel had learned his first lesson in survival and experienced his first flight with throngs of disorganized people through a prostrate country. When he finally came home to his wife and child, the Germans were already in Tarnow, but for eight days or so nothing much happened.

In a general way we know what the Nazis did to the Jews of Poland. We've read about the subject, seen exhibitions and films, and heard lectures. The fate of Tarnow was hardly different from that of hundreds and hundreds of other towns. Yet when Shmuel talks about it, he is not speaking generally about what happened to all the Jews, but about what happened to him, what he witnessed, what he did, how he feels about his own experiences.

During the first months, the killing and brutality in Tarnow seemed mostly disorganized, except for the humiliation and murder of the town's religious leaders. "They must have had a list," Shmuel mutters. The Gestapo arrested all the rabbis, cantors, religious judges, ritual slaughters and scribes, Hasidic rebbes and their followers, every religious functionary, with barely an exception. The Hasidim of the aging Stucziner Rebbe spirited him over the border to the Russian zone, where he died a natural death among his faithful.

First the Germans mocked and tortured the city's holiest Jewish men, brutally cutting their beards and sidelocks, beating them, kicking and jeering, making them wash the street on their hands and knees, stripping away their human dignity. Then after a day of amusement they herded them to the cemetery, stripped them, shot them and forced a group of Tarnow Jews to bury them. From the way he spoke of it, Shmuel might have been on the burial brigade. We could not bring ourselves to make sure.

The Nazis forced the *Kehilla*, the Jewish community, to organize senseless labor brigades moving stones back and forth from place to place, humiliating the men and paying them a meaningless pittance. Matters were not yet well organized. The brigades were often short-handed and then the Nazis would dragoon men from the streets at random. Sometimes they shot Jews who just happened to be out of doors, "for the fun of it," Shmuel spat out the sardonic words. It was dangerous to leave your house. This was before the Nazis crowded the Jews of Tarnow into a ghetto.

People owed Shmuel a lot of money. Before the war he had been in the coal and lumber business. He began to collect as much as he could. Most of his gentile customers paid but if they refused, he had no legal recourse. He gathered some 80,000 zlotys, he says, a great deal of money. With money you could hope to survive the German occupation.

Shmuel managed well enough before 1942, when they forced the Jews to live in a closed ghetto. He had money to buy food. Polish Christians operated a black market bartering food for jewels, furs, furniture, and other valuables. Of course the random killings didn't stop. The forced labor was better organized, so you couldn't avoid it, and they burned down the synagogues.

Shmuel brought the Tarnow Memorial Volume to one of our early sessions. It is a thick book, in Yiddish, written and compiled by survivors of the Holocaust from Tarnow, describing the life of the city's Jews, before they were murdered. There is a picture of the New Synagogue in the Tarnow Memorial Volume. It was an imposing white stone building with arched windows, and a high cupola. The interior view gives one a sense of awe and vastness. Four massive columns support the cupola, and an ornate arch, two stories tall dominates the eastern wall. Two golden lions crouch on a lintel over the ark, flanking the tablets of the Ten Commandments. Shmuel said that Tarnow lies in a valley and from the surrounding hills; the Synagogue and the Cathedral dominated the cityscape. In his childhood Shmuel heard about the construction of the New Synagogue. A local nobleman offered to pay half the cost of the construction if the community invited him to lay the cornerstone. The Jews of Tarnow accepted his generous offer and took back their earlier invitation to the Tzaddik of Sanz, a Hasidic leader. The Tzaddik was angry, not at the personal slight Shmuel assured us but because a gentile should not receive such an honor. He predicted that the synagogue wouldn't stand.

Sure enough it collapsed while the roof was being constructed, and it lay in ruins for more than ten years. When the Jews of Tarnow had once again collected enough money to reconstruct their synagogue, they invited the Tzaddik of Sanz to lay the cornerstone and the building stood, a source of pride to Tarnow's Jews, until the Nazis destroyed it.

The Nazis set fire to the synagogue and posted guards around it to stop the Jews from running in to save the twenty-five or thirty Torah scrolls that were in the ark. Only one Jew dared to go past the guards, Herman Weissman, the chief of the Jewish underworld in Tarnow. He emerged with two scrolls and escaped into the crowd, but the next day the Gestapo hunted him down and shot him in the street.

The Jewish underworld? Were there rings of Jewish thieves? "No" said Shmuel. "They were not thieves." They ran around with *shiksas* (non-Jewish women) and swindled peasants on market days. Weissman himself used to raise money for poor families who were ashamed to go to the *Kehilla* (the organized Jewish community) for relief. "This is the underworld?" Shmuel emphasized. "That's the point. That was like Jewish life was in Tarnow." He reverted to Yiddish to make his point: "The *gefil*; the *yiddisher gefil*." Then, Shmuel repeated it in English so we wouldn't miss the meaning: "a Jewish feeling." But the resonance of the word, "*gefil*" in Yiddish is just what Shmuel misses in Jewish life today.

Shmuel started talking about a friend of Weissman's who had a fruit stand in the market. His name was Tzalel (shortened and Yiddishized from Bezalel) and "he was a giant. I never knew his family name. They just called him Tzalel Big. His mouth! If he started talking the whole city heard what he wants. But he never harmed a worm. During the war he stood guard in front of the meetings of the *Kehilla*."

"One day is coming Amon Göth, the Kommandant of the Gestapo." Shmuel's anger boils up as he recalled the story and he slaps the arm of his chair: Göth arrested ten Jews and ordered each of them to round up fifty Jews from the city. Just to kill them. Five hundred people. Tzalel Big was one of the ten. He drank two liters of spirits, 96% alcohol, and came back roaring drunk to the Gestapo. "Amon Göth is waiting for them to come back. Where are your fifty Jews? he asked Tzalel. I got only one Jew. Where is your one Jew? That's me said Tzalel. He pulled open his shirt," Shmuel imitated the gesture "and Göth shot him on the spot." With a hint of admiration Shmuel was quiet again as he drummed the arms of his chair. "He was a brave man, and couldn't even write his name."

Then Shmuel remembered how Tzalel would shout a greeting to Shmuel's sister when she came to the market to do her shopping. "You could hear Tzalel all over the market. He would pick the best fruit for her and carry her basket home. A little child could hit him and he wouldn't do anything. That was the kind of man Tzalel was. He was not a religious man, just a Jew."

After the war Shmuel, told with some pride, that he saw Göth hanged on September 13, 1946, in Krakow. Shmuel took a special trip to see him executed. For Shmuel it was some combination of justice and revenge; perhaps just a way to bring closure to the memory.

The story about the market and Tzalel reminded Shmuel of the death of his mother. She had spent two years in Palestine with her daughter and returned to Poland in August 1939. "She was killed in the first segregation of the old people in a shocking way." Shmuel would start many of his stories with a provocative statement. When pressed, but not too hard, Shmuel hesitatingly went on to describe his mother's death in some detail.

"One day they selected 2,500 Jews over fifty years old. They said they were going to a special camp, and the Jews believed them. They took only the best clothes they had, jewelry, only as much as they could carry. They had to assemble in the market. It was ten o'clock in the morning. Shmuel spoke very softly. "Over 2,500 people. My mother, my sisters, and my two brothers-in-law."

At about two o'clock a few hundred SS men came and surrounded the market, setting up machine guns. "You can't get through. Who tried, he was killed. And then, after that they let in about a thousand. I can't believe it, Ukrainians, Latvians, and Letts. All drunk. You can't imagine how drunk. Drunk, *mishigga* drunk," Shmuel sighed but he continued with tears in his throat. They were armed with "hammers, axes, knives, anything else they could get. The Gestapo ordered the old people to undress and pile up all their belongings, which were carted away. Then they loosed the drunken men into the marketplace. And they started killing. Just like in a butchery, killing, cutting to pieces. I think that half of them just died of..." Shmuel didn't finish the sentence. Then after a few seconds he continued. "My mother was sick, heart trouble... I don't know if she was alive or dead. From the shock she died, you know. Two-thousand-five-hundred people were just cut to pieces like sausages."

The next day the Nazis organized a *Sonderkommando* of four hundred men, trucks and wagons. "We had to clean up," Shmuel said. He pointed to the photograph in the Tarnow Memorial book of the broad steps that led up to the market. "Blood ran down these steps for three days."

It's hard to fathom, and Shmuel comforted us, trying to convey the unreality of what he witnessed. "I'll tell you something. Till now, I don't understand. I see it with my own eyes. I don't know the expression to say it." He stumbled with his English vocabulary for a moment. "It happened but it didn't happen. I saw it but you can't believe it. I believe it, but I can't believe it. It's difficult to explain." He tried in Yiddish but the same words came out: *s'iz geshait, un is nisht geshait.*"

One of his nephews, whose mother was murdered in the market that day, hanged himself. For Shmuel suicide is an additional horror, not a useful response to the unreal and bizarre murders. The correct response in Shmuel's opinion was alertness. "I used my intuition and my brain." He placed his palm on his brow and added. "And I got a good one. I smelled danger. A thousand times I succeeded in avoiding danger, and I helped other people. I used my senses always, like a cat, on my feet. A thousand times I succeeded in living."

He gave an example of his ingenuity from the summer before the war. In the telling his eyes sparkled with pleasure at his resourcefulness.

One his older brothers, Yitzhak, found himself in a complex situation in the summer of 1939. He had fled Tarnow in 1918 to avoid military service, so he ended up with no Polish identity papers. After some wandering he found work in Berlin and rose to a highly responsible post in a chain of Jewish owned department stores; he married a wealthy German-Jewish woman and they had twin sons. In 1939 he and his family arranged to go to the United States. They had finished all the necessary preparations, but many Polish-born Jews had already been driven out of Germany in 1938 and others were in an increasingly untenable situation. So this part of the Braw family could not sail as they had planned. They left the twins in Berlin with their grandmother, because no children were then being rounded up Berlin. Yitzhak's wife went to Tarnow, but Yitzhak was unable to join her, because he was still technically a deserter from the Polish army. He went to Lvov where he hoped he would not be recognized.

Naturally Yitzhak's wife was despondent and frantically worried about her children. Shmuel thought of a way of spiriting them into Poland. "I have a plan" Shmuel told his sister-in-law. "But until I am sure we can do it, I won't tell what it is." He had a Christian friend, a man he'd gone to school with, who was serving in the border police. Shmuel thought that if the boys' grandmother brought them to the border, their mother could call out to them. They could race across the barrier and no one would stop them. Then his friend in the border police could have a few porters bring across their luggage. He approached his Christian friend and the man said, "It s a crazy idea but I like it. I like it, and I will do it." In addition to his bright idea Shmuel offered the man 500 Zlotys which must have made the plan a good deal more attractive. Everything went like clockwork; Shmuel's nephews were safe in Tarnow. "It was a nice swindle. Everybody in the city knew the story."

Even after the establishment of the ghetto, the Tarnow Jews did their best to spare the children. Shmuel takes some comfort in believing that they didn't know how dreadful the persecution was.

His daughter Esther attended the ghetto school. At first he told us that she was six years old at the time, being born in 1936. After some more thought Shmuel corrected himself. "She was born in 1932." So she was ten. Shmuel was quiet for a few seconds, reflecting on his daughter's fate.

"One day I came home from the forced labor..." Shmuel stopped and began the story differently and impersonally, from an emotional distance. "There was a well organized school in the ghetto in Tarnow where children went on learning just as if they were in their regular school." One day the Germans loaded the entire school into trucks, teachers and pupils. Prepared for that eventuality, the teachers distributed poisoned chocolates to the kids, allowing them to believe they were going on a picnic. The truck stopped in the woods near a convent in a forest a few kilometers away where Shmuel believes that the Nazis intended to shoot everyone. The soldiers opened the doors to find everyone dead already. "My daughter was in that transport" Shmuel said in a soft barely audible voice. So were his twin nephews, the only children of his brother Yitzhak who lacked Shmuel's ability to smell out danger. Yitzhak inadvertently delivered himself into the hands of the Gestapo in Lvov while he trying to trace a missing cousin.

He was killed there, and his wife was sent to Auschwitz. "Another family finished," Shmuel concluded.

Shmuel's story affected us deeply. We had read and heard similar accounts of death and murder, of children being poisoned and the horrors of the period. Sitting in an apartment in Jerusalem and listening to Shmuel tell and retell the story gave it immediacy for us. Only decades later, after the Holocaust, could we even think about the questions that the story evokes. How could they poison the children? It seems to be such an un-Jewish thing to do and Tarnow was such a Jewish place! Was there no chance for there to be at least one survivor? We thought about the decision itself and who made it. Whose plan was this to poison the children? Questions of all kinds remained, but the children and the teachers were dead.

By 1942, events had outpaced Shmuel's ability to help others to survive. On June 11th, 15th and 18th, the Nazis murdered 20,000 of Tarnow's Jews. "On one side were the graves of the Tzaddikim, you know, rabbis. They cleared the other side and dug eight graves, and you got another 20,000 lying in those eight graves. I haven't seen it, of course, but a friend of mine told me. The last few days, they just shot one layer like sardines, a bit at a time, a bit of earth another layer. And the earth was moving. They were still alive, a lot of them...still alive."

The closed ghetto was established in Tarnow on June 19, 1942, after that massacre. Some 20,000 Jews from Tarnow and the outlying areas were left in the city, densely packed into a few square blocks. The crowding was oppressive, four families to a room, strangers thrown together. No family life, no religious life, no personal life. In Shmuel's experience nothing could be maintained. On September 12, 1942 another 7,000 Jews were either killed on the spot or sent to Auschwitz. That was when Shmuel lost his wife. In the fall of 1942, he and five of his close friends escaped from the Ghetto.

The widow of one of Shmuel's employees, a gentile woman, hid them for a few days. Fearing discovery, the men headed east to the Soviet zone, traveling by night through the countryside where Shmuel had harvested timber for years. He knew his way perfectly. They met up with a band of partisans who were willing to accept Jews but unable to provide arms. They considered trying to buy guns, but they were afraid to linger in the German zone. The men waded across the river San to the Soviet side. Shmuel pondered and asked rhetorically, "What's the difference how you get killed."

The Russians didn't kill the men. They arrested them and tried them as German spies. "That was the irony" Shmuel commented. He and others were sent to a labor camp in Siberia and therefore missed the final stages of destruction of the entire community of Tarnow.

Chapter Three

"A City in My Bones"

Shmuel's stories kept returning to his youth and early adulthood in Tarnow. As a boy, Shmuel knew old people who were born in the first half of the nineteenth century. Through them his memories of Tarnow go back to the time when the city was a small town, more like the Poland the Jews first settled in, a medieval country, than the modernizing country in which Shmuel came of age.

Actually, Shmuel lived in quite a few places before moving to Israel. How well did he recall Tarnow, we asked? "I remember Tarnow more than any city in my life. It is a city in my bones, in my flesh." He expressed great love for his Tarnow. He described it as "a typical small city from the Jewish point of view." He referred to "the inner part of the city" and he meant the actual center of town as well as the spirit and heart of the place.

If you ask different people to describe their home towns, they will probably go about it in as many ways as there are people. Some will describe the climate, some will start with a historical event associated with the place, some will describe the landscape or well-known buildings in the town, and other might tell what is manufactured there. Shmuel had a different perspective on his home. "First thing, every city in Poland got *seine mishigoim*—its crazy people. We had more than two dozen. Every one of them was part of the city. You can't be without them. It is impossible for a city to exist without them!"

Older Rabbinic texts define a city as a place where there are at least ten idle people. Perhaps Shmuel's strong feeling of attachment to the mad folk of Tarnow springs from that ancient definition. Quite often Shmuel, who was not a particularly learned Jew, expressed opinions that reflected some passage from Jewish texts, but without direct reference to the written sources. The society in which he grew up was deeply imbued with the traditional patterns of Jewish life, which in turn were based on Jewish oral and written culture.

The Jewish people of Tarnow voluntarily supported their mad beggars. "You will call me a rebel again and I don't object" Shmuel added, returning to a private joke that we shared. "In my opinion, the people who gave the most were the poor and the middle classes. The rich people they only give if you call out their names in *shul*." Shmuel wipes his hand in a gesture of denigration.

Some of the mad men lived with their families; others took shelter in various public institutions, houses of study, bath houses, and the poor house. They would sleep in some communal building and wander the streets during the day. Shmuel remembered that they frequently said wise things, "like a philosophy," but the man he described at length was no wise fool.

Son of a well-known family, he had been shell-shocked in World War I. His name was Naftali Fleischer. "His brother owned a nice *gallanteries* shop. He would dress him in new clothes in the morning and at night he would come back home in *shmattas* (just rags). He gave the clothes away." Naftali went from door to door asking for pennies "to send to his poor auntie in another city. He would put the money in the mailbox, just like that, and stand next to it chanting, 'Its for my auntie, it's for my auntie, it's for my auntie.' Shmuel imitated the man's chant, clenching his fists and rocking back and forth like a man praying fervently. People tried to persuade Naftali to put the money in an envelope, but he would have none of it. And why did Jews keep giving him money? "Naftali just insisted, you couldn't turn him down."

Along with the madmen, the aged left a powerful impression on Shmuel while he was growing up. His mother had an uncle, for example, who died at the age of 112. He lived in a small village some twenty-five kilometers outside of Tarnow, and Shmuel made a point of visiting him whenever he could. He remembers a tiny man with a snow white beard, sitting in a high chair with a velvet yarmulke on his head. Whenever a visitor came, he would tell the unmarried daughter who kept house for him to bring him a hat, commenting on the difference between gentiles, who take off their hats to honor guests and Jews, who put them on. She had to announce his visitors, for he was blind during the last thirty years of his life. Shmuel told us that once she announced unexpected guests—*ungerecht* in Yiddish. Shmuel took the word in another sense and said that, on the contrary, everyone was righteous—*gerecht*. Shmuel regarded him as a saint, and he was well-known and widely venerated in the region.

Although he was blind and never left his house in the village, Shmuel's great uncle somehow knew when any of his relatives passed away. Upon the death of Shmuel's grandmother, the old man announced to his daughter: 'Sister has gone home.' After that, and contrary to Jewish custom, he never again mentioned her, or any other deceased relation. For Shmuel, his centenarian relative represented a way of life that no longer existed. Supported by another of his daughters who manufactured brooms in Krakow, the old man lived in tranquility, surrounded by his children, grandchildren, and great-grandchildren. Every evening five or six of his progeny would gather in his home to study Torah. In fact the death of his son followed a difference of opinion about a passage in one of the Torah commentaries.

The father, who was then 105, told his eighty year old son he was in error. The son disagreed. An argument ensued and finally the father said, 'If you look in such and such a book, you will see that I am right .' He sent his son off to check the reference, "And he never came back." Shmuel was likely unaware of the grotesque humor in the story he was recounting. The old man lived in a dilapidated wing of the family's wooden house. When his aged son took down the book, a section of the roof fell in on his head and killed him. Shmuel said, he never mentioned him after that.

What had Shmuel talked to the old man about on his frequent visits? Did he ask him personal questions, hoping to profit by his accumulated wisdom? "No I wouldn't bother him with anything like that." The old man apparently lived in a world of his own, unaware of what went on outside the walls of his wooden house. He would feel Shmuel's face and reproach him for not letting his beard and earlocks grow, but otherwise he had little to say to Shmuel. He was simply a presence connected to an even more impressive presence, a father of legendary piety who frequently prayed outside in his garden, rather than in the synagogue with his fellow Jews, seeking contact with God through nature. That must have been in the early nineteenth century, within living memory of the Ba'al Shem Tov, the founder of the Hasidic movement.

Shmuel's aged uncle died, appropriately enough, on the very day Hitler invaded Poland. Shmuel also told us about his grandfather, another member of that generation whose life began in the first third of the nineteenth century. In contrast to his tiny, frail, blind brother-in-law Shmuel's grandfather was a gigantic man of severe mien who went about with a heavy walking stick. Shmuel confided to us that he was never afraid of the old man. "He raised the stick, but he never touched you. He was making a noise, but he never did anything to you. A minute later he was smiling like nothing happened."

He and his wife had sixteen children, of whom only seven survived to adulthood. One son took over his father's butcher shop, "a marvelous business." By today's standards, he was a fanatically religious man, although not abnormally pious in comparison with the rest of Polish Jewry at the time. He was famous for taking a financial loss rather than sell meat with the slightest suspicion that it might not be strictly kosher. He always rose before dawn to recite his morning prayers at sunrise with other particularly pious men and regularly went to the ritual bath. During World War I, Shmuel's grandparents refused to flee to Hungary with his father and family. Shmuel put these words in his mouth: "I'm not going from my background. If they kill me, that is God's wish. I have to be killed. I'm here, and I'm staying here." Fortunately he and his wife survived the war. She was a saintly woman, "She never raised her voice," Shmuel said.

The tall, vigorous, impressive retired butcher in his long, black coat and his broad-trimmed, black felt weekday hat or his luxurious, fur *shtreimel* on Shabbat, a bearded patriarch with his heavy staff, must have loomed large in Shmuel's imagination as a child. His father too wore traditional Hasidic clothes all week long; only on the Sabbath did he wear the elaborate black, silk caftan. Shmuel felt that such figures no longer existed in the world. To his eyes even the pious Jews of Jerusalem's Meah Shearim didn't seem genuine. They lacked the qualities Shmuel remembers in the old men of Tarnow. For Shmuel, piety was not to be found in costume but in the inner qualities expressed in behavior.

Before World War I, Shmuel's family lived in a large house with a big yard and stables. His father kept powerful work horses to draw wagons full of timber from the estates where his workmen felled trees. As he described the house, a memory came to Shmuel. One Sunday when the Christian stable-hands had the day off he rode one of the horses as his father walked them down to the nearby river to water them. Shmuel was about six years old at the time. "Horses like to lie down in the water," he explained to us. Absent-mindedly his father let the horse wade into the river with Shmuel on the horse's back. "In one second he lay down, and I was in the water. That's it!" He didn't bother telling us the obvious: that his father waded in and pulled him out of the water.

Smiling shrewdly, Shmuel announced: "When I was born, I was a *mamzer*" (a bastard). What was one to make of that kind of blunt statement? According to

Jewish tradition a *mamzer* is an offspring of an illegal marriage, or an adulterous union. If Shmuel was born a *mamzer*, he would still be a *mamzer*—the status is permanent according to Jewish law. But he clearly wasn't! Shmuel simply enjoyed catching his listener's attention by making provocative statements and then telling his story.

Shmuel's parents, like most of the Jews of Galicia, were married only by a rabbi, and they never bothered to enter their marriage in the civil registry. A *ketuba* (a Jewish marriage contract) was good enough for them. The children went officially by their mothers' family name. However, during the First World War, many of the Jewish men were drafted and their wives couldn't collect the soldier's allotment without a civil marriage certificate, especially if they were refugees in other places. So many Galician Jews got married civilly. Shmuel remembers going with his younger brother to see his parents get married. By then of course, his parents already had grandchildren, the children of their older daughters. He recalled walking with his parents to the registry office and witnessing his parents' civil marriage.

Shmuel described his father as a devout Jew and an astute businessman whom everyone respected. Although he could read and write only the Hebrew alphabet, he spoke perfect grammatical Polish. He was a calm, firm, and authoritative man who got his way without unnecessary conflict. When he bought something, he never bargained. He asked the merchant whether he was making a fair profit and took the man's word. "He never got cheated twice. He just wouldn't go back there." In all his years in business he never became involved in a lawsuit. He always chose to settle out of court rather than be required to take an oath before the civil authorities, something which might have violated his religious principles.

His father was a follower of the Szabner rebbe, a Hasidic Rabbi, who lived in the same building as Shmuel's family after World War I. It was a large structure built around a courtyard with stores, workshops, and storerooms on the ground floor and apartments up above. They had hot and cold running water, a modern luxury in Tarnow.

Although Shmuel's family had a housekeeper and a laundress who came in every week or so, his mother did all the cooking. Every night she would prepare the food for the following day, and on Thursday nights she would get up early, at one or two o'clock in the morning, so that by Friday morning at five o'clock everything would be ready for Shabbat. During the week days she worked as the cashier in the retail outlet of her husband's business.

Could she speak Polish well too? "No," Shmuel answered emphatically and he was reminded of his mother's defective Polish grammar. He explained that Polish numbers are inflected for gender, and his mother could never see the point of getting them straight. Once when he corrected her for using the wrong form of the number two, she said, "Tell me, is the other one more than two? Is that what you went for years to school to learn?" "In her mind" Shmuel explained, "that's a two and that's a two. What's the difference?"

Was Shmuel mother a religious woman? "Of course" Shmuel responded. What kind of question was that? How could she fail to be religious? Her father was a "*mishigineh* Hasid." What did he mean by calling him *mishigineh*? Did he think the Hasidim were crazy? He dodged the question, tacitly acknow- ledging that he really didn't mean "crazy." In Poland, he explained, "eighty percent of the Jews were strictly religious. Today you would say there were fanatics. But they were not fanatics then. They were simple, plain, religious people, but to the dot. No compromises. Nothing. *Shabbos* (the Sabbath), *yontif* (holidays), Kosher, *milchig* (dairy), *fleishig* (meat), everything—to the dot. That was religious. They weren't fanatics."

A prosperous business in a community like Tarnow had both status and responsibilities. Most of the Jews were appallingly poor. *Tzedakah*, charity, was both a human impulse and a formal Jewish obligation. Shmuel remembers his father's generosity. "Of course he had what to give. If a poor man, say an un-employed garment worker, came into the shop and said, 'I haven't got a *shabbos*,' the shopkeeper would generally give him a few zlotys, or he would quickly raise some money among his friends. A man and his family had to be able to celebrate *shabbos* with challah, fish, wine and a little meat, even the poorest man."

Shmuel's father also gave to other people, whose case was the opposite. They earned enough for *shabbos*, but not for the rest of the week. They would borrow money on Sunday and return it on Friday. Shmuel remembered that his father asked one of them to forget it. Why not keep the money, since he was going to borrow it right back? The man refused, because he didn't want to assume the halachic responsibilities of someone who guards another's property over the Sabbath. Finally there were a large number of poor families, whom they permitted simply to run up bills for coal, knowing their chances of collecting were slim. But that's a more dignified way of helping people.

All of this of course was in addition to the official charitable institutions of the local Jewish community and the special public appeals that might be made through the rebbes and their courts. Shmuel was not actually singling out his father for behaving exceptionally. A Jew with wherewithal simply did not turn away a Jew who needed money or support, not in Tarnow at any rate, at least not according to Shmuel's construction of the past.

When Shmuel praised Jews for their generosity, he mentioned poor Jews or exceptional Jews like the doctor who not only refused to take money from the poor but also gave them money to buy the medicines he prescribed! Shmuel claimed that the rabbis in Poland were among the poorest people of the community, yet, "if you gave them twenty pennies, they would put away ten for *tzedaka*." He recalled a close friend, "He was killed. He was a *zaygermacher*, a watchmaker. You know, I haven't seen in my life a poorer man than this man." Yet when an old woman brought her clock in for repair, the only valuable thing she owned, he couldn't bring himself to charge her, even as much as he had to pay for the parts. 'What could I do?' he asked Shmuel. 'I know she didn't have the five zlotys to pay for it.' Shmuel concluded: "He was a real *tzaddik*."

Most of the Jews of Tarnow lived in great need. Shmuel remembers the poverty in the community and he described it graphically. Many people lived for years with no hope of improvement, a whole family in a single small room with a couple of chairs, a couple of straw mattresses against the walls, and two sewing machines in the middle. The father and mother worked from the moment they lit the *havdala* candle, marking the end of the Sabbath, and they couldn't make "one and one equal two." Shmuel said for their Sabbath they might get one half a kilo of meat and a little bread. They might have one pair of shoes for all their children, passed down from child to child until the leather fell apart. "When you came into a home like that" Shmuel summed up, "when it's cold and wet, it smells. The children are covered with just rags. They are shivering. If you don't have a feeling for that, then you are only a piece of wood."

Yet Shmuel insisted that the Jews of Tarnow were happy in a way that few are happy today. "They suffered," he admitted, "but they were happy because they were *tsofriden*, content." They worried daily about *parnossa*, making a living, and by that they meant merely making it from one Sabbath to another.

When Shmuel talks about the Sabbath in Tarnow it is his tone rather that his words that communicate his meaning. His voice softens and he chants the words. Even the poorest people had enough to eat on the Sabbath. In every synagogue there was a little fish and spirits for Kiddush (a snack after religious services) in the morning and *Shalosh Seudis* (the ritual third Sabbath meal) in the afternoon. For one day people stopped worrying about making a living. They got real rest, *Shabbos menucha*. Nowhere since then has Shmuel experienced such complete repose.

Religious Jews have always done more or less the same things on the Sabbath. The women prepare dinner and light candles; the men go to the synagogue, families sing hymns at the table and people visit each other. The ceremonial acts that one is required to perform and the work that one is forbidden to do together give an Orthodox Jewish Sabbath a shape recognizable the world over.

The Hasidim have a reputation for heightening the fervor of their religious observance with alcohol. Shmuel described Tarnow as predominantly Hasidic. Did the Jews there drink a lot on *shabbos*? What about the spirits that were served in the synagogues? Shmuel readily admitted that the Jews drank, sometimes a lot, especially on Purim and Simchat Torah. Shmuel added: "But I never saw a drunk Jew. If a Jew had too much to drink he would just go home slowly and go to bed." (Indeed, one of the traditional occupations of Jews in Galicia was to run taverns.) Returning to drinking on the Sabbath, Shmuel admitted that they drank a lot on Shabbat too. But where did they drink, was it at home or in the synagogue? "No" Shmuel answered with a smile "in pubs." He repeated it again since he saw by our expression that we found it difficult to believe him. Did Jews really go to gentile bars and purchase drinks on *shabbos*? Shmuel explained: "First, Jews had their own pubs in Tarnow. Second they were buying tickets on Friday, so on Saturday they could get drinks without paying. And if they got any left, on Sunday they can get their money back."

Were these the religious Jews that Shmuel had described so often? The Hasidim of Tarnow, with *shtreimels* and long black *kapotas* (coats) in bars on the Sabbath? "Of course." Shmuel emphasized. "Most of them." We couldn't picture a tavern full of black-coated bearded Hasidim whiling away the Sabbath with drinks. So we pressed: On Shabbat a Hasid would go out to a bar and drink like a goy? "Like a goy," Shmuel concurred. Then he quickly corrected himself. "They didn't feel like a goy. They felt like a Jew."

He described a kind of free lunch in the taverns, "broad beans, very fresh ones. They cooked them on Friday and kept them in big pots with a cover, over a lamp to keep them hot. And that was nothing. They were sitting and eating and drinking beer. Not like goyim. Goyim were not drinking. Goyim were *shikkers* (drunks). Jews were sitting for a couple hours. Then they went to Mincha (afternoon prayer service) in the *shuls*. They had some schnapps for *Shalosh Seudis*. Then they came back to the pub and had another beer.

We guessed that was mainly in the winter, thinking of the cold freezing weather in Poland, gales sweeping out of the forests and scouring the desolate, rutted streets full of frozen mud. Shmuel was quick to correct that, "they drank in winter and summer." It was obvious that our preconceptions of life in the town of Tarnow were inconsistent with Shmuel's reconstruction. And ours was the romanticized version! Shmuel was surprised by our surprise. "It was just a normal way of life" in Tarnow when he was a young man, Shmuel repeated.

What did the women do on the Sabbath while their husbands were sitting around in bars? Shmuel explained that they usually went visiting other women. He couldn't remember seeing a Jewish woman in a bar. "Seldom a woman drinks spirits," he reassured us.

As for the men's conversations on those convivial Sabbath afternoons, it was mainly, "stories about rabbis, and some politics. But it wasn't worth a penny, the politics. Just stories."

For the men, the *mikvah*, the ritual bath, on Friday morning was generally part of the preparation for the Sabbath. In fact, Shmuel's father, like other very religious men, went to the *mikvah* daily. Shmuel went only three times a week, on Sundays, Tuesdays, and Thursdays, when the water was changed. Cleanliness was more important to him than ritual purity. He would go with his father, almost always arriving at a time when the water was warm enough, but not yet too hot. But once Shmuel's father, who never wore a watch but was nevertheless uncannily punctual, got up about seven minutes late. By the time they got to the bathhouse, the *mikvah* was hotter than Shmuel was used to. He was just getting ready to brave it when an emaciated old man rushed in, slipped out of his clothes in a few seconds, and plunged into the water, skin, bones and some grey hair. As soon as he got into the water up to his neck, the old man cried out in distress, and Shmuel was worried. His father made a reassuring sign, nothing was the matter. The skinny old man shouted again. He was calling the attendant. "The *mikvah* was boiling and he was shivering. Give him some more steam! He needs more steam." Shmuel laughed out loud at the picture he had called to mind. That morning Shmuel put back on his clothes without immersing.

Tarnow was full of synagogues: from tiny *shtibelach* (analogous to storefront churches in American cities), through small but well-established *shuls*, and the *shuls* associated with various Hasidic rebbes in town, some in impressive buildings, to the large, imposing synagogue of the official organized Jewish community, the *Kehillah*. As Shmuel evoked them, the synagogues appeared to be at the center of Jewish fellow-feeling. He claimed that anywhere in Poland, wherever an unknown Jew showed up in a synagogue, after prayers, the men would gather around him and questions him. "Where is the Jew from? What brings you here? Can we help you?"

The men's social life revolved around their *shuls*. Those with spare time would study together there. "There was nothing to distract them." But of course the instrument that helped the Jews maintain themselves in a hostile environment also exerted enormous social pressure inwards on the men who frequented them. You had to dress and behave like a pious person. They checked up on you. Since Shmuel's family lived in the same building as the Szabner Rebbe, Rabbi Shlomo David Unger, Shmuel never left the house without a hat or a cap, although he admitted to removing it and stuffing it in his pocket when he got out of sight. Naturally the rebbe would check whether Shmuel was wearing his *tzitzis* (ritual fringes as an undergarment) as well. Another Rebbe, the Shtutziver, would not ask Shmuel whether he had put on his tefillin (his phylacteries) in the morning. Instead he asked, 'Are your tefillin still kosher.'

Shmuel spoke with fondness of this interference with his life. However, he had a younger brother who joined Hashomer Hatzair, a left wing Zionist youth organization, and ran off to Palestine at the age of eighteen. His brother's memories would probably be less fond of the rebbes and the orthodoxy in Tarnow.

How did the Braw family celebrate holidays, particularly the major family holiday of Passover when Shmuel was growing up? Shmuel was clear: "Every year the same." Did his grandfather, the tall butcher, make a big Seder for all of his children and their families? "It wasn't like that in Poland. Everybody made a Seder by himself." Rarely would Shmuel's married brothers and sisters come to his father's house for a holiday meal.

Shmuel's memories were triggered and began pouring back. Shmuel explained: Days before Pesach there was a "revolution" in Tarnow's Jewish neighborhoods. People brought all their furniture out into the street so they could clean house better. They changed the straw in their mattresses. They had their houses painted, at least the kitchens if not the whole apartment. Shmuel remembered how they would paint the walls one color and then add a pattern resembling wall paper in a contrasting color with special rollers. One sees paint jobs similar in old houses in Jerusalem. And Shmuel often helped friends and relatives paint their houses in Jerusalem as well.

Shmuel had told us of the dire poverty of most Jews in Tarnow. Did the poor also have their houses prepared for Pesah? They would hire gentile day laborer to whitewash the kitchens. Middle class Jewish families had live-in Jewish servants and gentile peasant girls from the surrounding communities. A housewife would assign the heavy work to the maid but she would clean the kitchen herself. No Christian could be relied on to achieve the meticulous standards of cleanliness required to prepare a house Kosher for Passover. In Shmuel's view, nowhere do Jews today clean as thoroughly as Jews in Poland did for Passover.

"The Hasidim were not *mishigineh* like here. They were ordinary, nice people, but serious ones. They did just what God said." Even ignorant Jews who said their prayers by rote without understanding a word knew exactly what had been done in the past. "They remembered, *Zaide* (grandpa) did it this way. *Bubbe* (grandma) did it that way. And they carried on the tradition without asking questions."

Did Shmuel's family have a special set of dishes for Pesah? Shmuel pretends to take offense. "How can you ask a question like that? Everybody in Tarnow had special dishes. Even the poorest ones."

Shmuel's father dressed in a snow white *kittel*, a robe reserved for the most solemn of ritual occasions such as Yom Kippur and for the Seder on Pesah. He reclined "on the bed that I was sleeping in." The whiteness of everything stuck in Shmuel's mind, and he recounted his impressions with awe and veneration.

His father ate only *shmura* matzah, matzah made from flour ground from wheat which has been especially set aside and supervised from the time of its sowing, to prevent any possibility of natural leavening at any point in the process. The matzah in Tarnow was all hand-made. Bakers had special ovens and workrooms used only on Pesah. One of Shmuel's brothers-in-law came from a village near Tarnow and owned a matzah bakery. The whole extended family sometimes went out there on the Sunday before Pesah to bake matzah. They shared expenses proportionally and Shmuel said they sang all day as they baked. They were not allowed to eat the matzah before the Passover Seder but there was surely temptation to do so. They did make up one batch of egg matzah, which was not the same as plain matzah and they could eat that.

Shmuel said that his family in Tarnow very much enjoyed Pesah and its elaborate preparations. Even his mother enjoyed the holiday but it was a lot of work, especially for the women in the households.

The annual High Holidays, Rosh Hashanah and Yom Kippur also returned vividly in Shmuel's memories. Shmuel's father used to lead the morning prayers in his synagogue on Yom Kippur. As a boy Shmuel would go and stand by his father's side as he sang the prayers in front of the whole congregation. In the afternoon, Shmuel went to the large community synagogue, where he sang in the choir.

Every year for the High Holidays, Shmuel's older brother Yitzhak would come back to Tarnow from Berlin, where he was known as Ignatz. He would stay until the end of Succoth (about a month). Shmuel recalled asking him once why he came back. After all, Yitzhak was a wealthy man. He could afford to take a vacation anywhere. And he was no longer a completely observant Jew. He ate only kosher food, but his job demanded that he work on Saturdays and he did, seldom managing to attend religious services in the synagogue. Yitzhak's answer was that the only way he could cope with the sterile, gentile and latently hostile atmosphere of Germany for eleven months of the year was by returning to Jewish Tarnow for one month. At least that was how Shmuel remembered it.

Yitzhak prayed at the court of the Shtutziner Rebbe who was an awesomely handsome man according to Shmuel. His eyes showed the man's refined soul, the soul of one who seems far elevated above this earth.

The court of the Shtutziner Rebbe was far from the only one in Tarnow. After the devastation of World War I, Hasidic leaders from rural towns had moved to the city. Thousands of Hasidic Jews flocked to Tarnow from all over Galicia to be in their Rebbe's presence for the holidays. At *Tashlich*, a picturesque ceremony performed on the first day of Rosh Hashanah in which Jews symbolically empty their pockets to cast their sins into a body of water, all the town's traffic stopped dead. The streets were clogged with black-coated Jews on their way to the riverbank, led by their rebbes in their entire splendor.

"The whole city was in one spot," Shmuel said. It was a spectacle not to be missed even by the gentiles.

During the eight days of Succoth the Shtutziner's *shul* was packed. His dramatic ceremonial processions around the synagogue with *lulav* and *etrog* (palm branches and citrons) and the Torah scrolls, raised his followers to religious ecstasy. At its height he would lie weeping on the floor. After that and the exuberant joy of Simchat Torah, Yitzhak would leave Tarnow for Berlin inspired, ready to face another cold year as Ignatz.

Somewhat surprised at himself Shmuel said: "I am still living half in that life." He occasionally finds himself sitting down and losing himself in his memories of childhood and young adulthood. "I sit down and say to myself, I'm in Israel, and my thoughts are forty years back. I remember a lunch, a gathering. You know, it's coming to me. That was a normal life, every day, every week the same, with some changes. You know that is amazing. Explain it to me. Sometimes I can put it away in my head and forget it." And then with a slight pause he says, "I remember everything about Tarnow." He conceded that there were other attractive Jewish communities in Poland, "but mine Tarnow was to me the nicest. I'm not praising myself or the city. I met after the war a lot of people who asked me where I am from. I said, Tarnow, and they said; now that was a nice town. It is a little town, 60,000 people, 30,000 Jews. What are 30,000 people? That is nothing. But it was 30,000 *typical* Jews. In every way, *typical* Jews," emphasizing to us the ordinary and the typical.

Even when our discussions with Shmuel extended beyond a reasonable hour at night, he continued to remind himself of stories that he wanted us to hear. He started telling about the *frachters* of Tarnow, messengers, men who took letters and packages from Tarnow to Krakow, sometimes money to be deposited in a bank or paid to a creditor. The *frachters* were generally simple men. Theirs was not a learned profession. Yet one of them, Zalman Maurer, wrote a book. It was called, *Sei Nisht Zee Gut Yingle* (Don't be too good, lad). "A *frachter* from Tarnow wrote a book" Shmuel reiterated.

And with one foot out the door one evening, he recalled another person, Menachem Brandwein, the retired owner of a shoe factory, a learned Jew, used to sit and study Talmud on *Shabbos*, smoking a cigar! Everybody knew that smoking was strictly forbidden on the Sabbath. The explanation of this most aberrant behavior appealed to Shmuel and it was short. Some observant Jews used to blow smoke into a box on Friday and inhale it on Shabbat. Brandwein saw that as hypocritical, just as bad as smoking a lighted cigar. So he smoked a cigar on the Sabbath. Tarnow had its characters, and not all of them were Hasidim or observant Jews.

"If you are rich, not rich but wealthy," Shmuel said, "you got it and you are used to that. You think it's a normal thing. But if you lose it, you start to feel what you lost. We had diamonds at home, and we lost them. Diamonds. We never got them back."

Chapter Four

"A Shtinkindike Shtik Flaish"

The strongest and most vivid memories that Shmuel was able to share involved three parts of his life: the Holocaust, the vanished world of Tarnow, and his experiences in Siberia. He was ready to talk about Jerusalem, Melbourne and of course his two daughters, but he was eager to preserve his memories of Tarnow, his deep emotional responses to loss and horror of the Holocaust, and his success in surviving imprisonment in Siberia. Indeed, some of Shmuel's frequent nightmares were memories of Siberia. The subject of his experiences in Siberia often floated to the surface or was dragged up in association with a point Shmuel was making about something else. He repeatedly found himself thinking about what he underwent in the camps.

Sometimes he depreciated his own suffering. He owns a book in Yiddish about Treblinka which obsesses him: the dogs trained to snap the genitals off men on their way to be gassed, and the monstrous executioners who specialized in braining infants. "Compared to that, what happened to me was nothing," he said, emphatically, his eyes brimming. "That is the difference between the Germans and the Russians. The Germans will shoot you, but the Russians say they don't have to shoot you. They just let you fade away. Your life is worth nothing to them. "After all," Shmuel reflected, "You got 250,000,000 Russians..." Abruptly Shmuel interrupted himself and began telling how one evening, after a day of forced labor; the guard came around to recruit sixty men for a special job. They would have to work all night, but they would get the following day off, plus 100 grams of sugar, 100 grams of tobacco, a double portion of bread, and even a bit of meat." Shmuel didn't want to volunteer, but he happened to be an expert lumberman because of his experience in the family business. He was not allowed to refuse. The camp authorities threatened to lock him up in what he calls the '*carcer*' so he agreed to go out and supervise the special brigade.

When he got there, he told us: "First thing, I refused to work. That's the difference between the Germans and the Russians. In Russia you can swear to them. You can refuse. They won't kill you." But why did Shmuel first agree to leave the camp with the crew and then refuse to work? Shmuel enjoyed creating suspense. "The officer is coming and asked me why I refused to work. I told him because I know this work, and the rope is too thin. It was dangerous. They were cutting and hauling timber on a hill, and if the rope broke, two and a half ton logs would roll down. Everybody on the floor is finished."

The officer threatened to lock Shmuel up, but Shmuel was unmoved. "I told him, 'okay, but don't say I didn't warn you. I told you the truth.'" So one had the right to demand a decent rope in the camps? "Of course I'm not killing people!"

Shmuel's stubbornness won his comrades some time to rest while the Russians went back to get a stronger rope. It finally arrived and they had to start working. "The weather was freezing maybe forty-five below zero, but when you work, you get hot. You can't work in the clothes what they gave you." Shmuel described the crude quilted cotton coats they were issued, ungainly garments that were too heavy to move about in. Shmuel and some other prisoners left their coats in a pile on the ground while they worked.

"The guards had built a great bonfire. They are warming themselves, and we are working. It was a windy night and some embers blew onto the pile of coats. It's cotton and it starts burning, slowly, slowly. When I took it up, I had a hole as big as my hand. It was not only myself, it was four of them." Back in the camp Shmuel and the other men were brought before an officer to be sentenced for destroying government property. "The officer took a piece of paper smaller than my finger." Shmuel held up his pinky. "He said to me, 'That piece of paper is worth more than you four.' I said, 'I understand?'" Shmuel's voice took on the arrogant officer's harsh tone: "'What do you understand?' 'I'll tell you what I understand. That is Communism!' "And he looks at me. 'How dare you say that!' 'All right, teach me how to say it another way. If you say that that piece of paper is worth more than four people, that is Communism. That is one hundred percent Communism!'"

Shmuel would have stopped telling the story at that point. He had explained the difference between Russians and Germans. But how did the story end? The men were charged with sabotage. "I was working. He was sitting by the fire. He *made* the fire. I get ten days *carcer*. Instead of rest, I had to go to jail! But another boss, the working boss, said, 'If you don't take him out and let him work, thirty people from every brigade won't be able to work. You got no wood tomorrow. Forget it.'" So Shmuel, who just happened to be an expert logging foreman, and who just happened to he able to exploit a conflict between the disciplinary branch of the camp and the productive branch, was released.

Shmuel's experience in Siberia taught him that labor camps are representative of Soviet society, not sadistic, but cruelly indifferent to human life. The Russians weren't arrogant like the Nazis. You could argue with the officers. "You could swear at them too because we hadn't to fear for our lives. Our lives were worth nothing. Nothing. You're rubbish. Just a piece of rubbish. Nothing. Not even worth murdering." He assumes that he was sent to Siberia because of the severe labor shortage in the USSR: not because the system was diabolical, but because it considered slave labor as another productive resource.

Shmuel learned the nature of the Soviet system step by step. After he and his companions were stopped on the Russian side of the river San, he was detained and interrogated. At that point he was still relieved to have escaped the Nazi occupation, and he expected to be released. "When I was first called out from the jail, the first night, it was nothing. Just writing my name, where I got family. He asks a few questions, says, 'That's enough for the day.' He rings the bell and soldiers take me away. When is coming the third and fourth night, and I always answer the same, so he starts to get mad." Suddenly Shmuel stood up, "You like to stand four hours like that?" he asked demonstrating. He stood flush against the wall with his face, his chest, his arms, his thighs, and his toes touching it. Then he stepped back and turned around. Vehemently he continued, still smarting at the injustice, "Four hours he was sitting and smoking. One move, with the hand, and he's behind you. He says, don't move or I'll kill you. Every night, three or four hours, because I didn't give him the right answers." Shmuel sat down and corrected himself: "I give him the right answers, but he wants a lie, just put in a lie. Who sent me, which government? You are a spy. You are an enemy of the Russian people. You want to destroy the Russian army. You are a capitalist.

"I said to him one night, 'Listen, you are wasting your time, because I have nothing more to say to you. What do you want me to say, a story?'" For ten or eleven nights Shmuel stuck to the truth. The interrogations lasted all night, and he was not permitted to sleep during the day. Guards watched him through the peephole in his cell door and roused him whenever he began to doze off. He grew weaker and weaker. At last another prisoner, a Jew from the Ukraine who "spoke a beautiful Russian," set him straight. He told Shmuel, "I got an advice to you. Go up today and make them a surprise. Tell them you'll sign everything. They'll be very happy.'

Shmuel still didn't want to admit that the Polish government had sent him to spy on Russia, an utter falsehood, but he needed to sleep. When the interrogator said, 'For the last time, will you sign?' Shmuel said, "Yes." He imitated the Russian soldier's delighted repetition of his "Yes?" for us, almost singing it. "He couldn't believe it," Shmuel explained. "He asked if I'm hungry. He'll give me some bread. I said, 'I'm not hungry, only tired. I want to sleep.' He said, 'You will sleep.' He was happy, you see. He'd done his job. He found a spy. The spy was sentenced to five years of hard labor with no trial. "In Russia there is only a trial if they want to show something."

After sentencing, Shmuel was sent to a collection point with a large number of other prisoners who would also be sent to Siberia. Six or seven hundred men were gathered in a crowded hall of some kind. "You haven't got room where to sit down. Three days and three nights standing. No water. No nothing. Like living in a sewer. It stinks. It is hot. You are wet. You are standing or lying on each other." He described the experience with indignant disgust as if he were again in that sweltering room. "And they feed us" he continued sarcastically. "How you try to get to the door even to get a bit of water?"

Shmuel's anger is fresh as if the event had just occurred. "You can't get rid of it. That is something that is not happening in the history of mankind. It's impossible."

The prisoners formed an indistinct mob. No one knew anyone else. "Just sheep," Shmuel called them. Mostly people spent their time "quarreling." He continued: "They got nothing else in mind but to get five centimeters more room. The rest doesn't exist. You don't think about washing. You don't think about eating. Nothing."

The prisoners helped each other somewhat. "Yes, but not a hundred percent. Some people haven't got it. I don't know in English how to say it, *a selbstgefil fun menchhait.* They become animals. It's an experience that makes you lose a sense of humanity. That's it. That's the right words. You forget that you are a human being. First thing we haven't expected that they keep us three days and three nights! We are sure that, seven hundred people, in two hours, they will take us out. But nothing happened. They forgot about us." The people near the door kept pounding on it so that it would be opened every once in a while to let in a breath of air. From time to time detainees would faint. No one knew how long they would be locked in. How could they plan an intelligent course of action in those circumstances?

According to Shmuel, the most debilitating aspect of life as a prisoner in the USSR was neither the harsh physical environment nor the loss of freedom in itself. The need for constant alertness took the heaviest toll. "Every second danger could come. You get weak, not from work. Because you got to be all the time on your toes. Even at night you have to think." Shmuel quickly figured out that the only way to survive in the crowded detention hall was to keep calm and avoid squabbles. "If you start, you see, quarreling, if there are two, it builds up and up. They never stop. But if one doesn't answer, it goes down and down and down. I remember exactly. I was in a corner, and I was lucky, because I haven't got nobody behind me. I can lean on the wall." Shmuel started organizing the men around him. "If you say, 'Calm down,' it's not much, but it helps a little. You have to be still and not move. If you move, you get hotter. You annoy yourself and the people next to you."

"I'm not praising myself. In every place, situation like this one, my mind was a hundred percent more than normal. My mind was working like a blitz. Sometimes it works."

Shmuel never seemed to be inventing adventures or exaggerating his own role in events to make an impression on us. You could compare him to a child on a roller coaster: if he hadn't imagined he was driving the careening vehicle, he would have been too terrified to remain in it. As he told us his story, Shmuel accounted for his survival by attributing it to intuition and cleverness and the will and the energy he possessed to stay alive, never letting up for a moment.

After being sentenced to the labor camp he was sent to Siberia in a slow train that kept stopping to pick up more deportees. The prisoners were transported in crowded boxcars. In jail they had lived on bread and water. In the train they barely had that. Late one night the guards threw open the doors of the train and five or six soldiers lugged in a huge cauldron of barley, cooked in oil. "Can you eat it? It's so hot, and you can't take it. And another thing, you got forty people in the wagon and four plates. And you had to eat it quick, because he's going from one wagon to another one. So I have seen what's going on. I said to myself, 'That's impossible.' Because the first one that's taking a bite, he burned his tongue. I said to myself, 'I've got to eat this barley, what can I do?' So I got a *casquette*, you know, a cap, a winter cap, and I open it quick. I come to the door with my cap and the soldier who, the cook looks at me and then I understand later what he said. He said, '*mologiets.*' You know what '*mologiets*' means? It means, 'That's a clever boy.' And he put on a full one!" Shmuel's voice rang out with triumph as he told this part of the story. "You know, maybe three liters. I wait till it gets cold, and I got a cake." He clapped his hands with pleasure. "And I eat all night long. I share with somebody. I was quick. In the next three days it was the same. It was normal to them. If the people didn't eat it, they would give it away. Other people followed Shmuel's example, benefiting from his cleverness.

Once he was in the camp Shmuel's presence of mind couldn't get him extra food. He says that Siberia was worse than Nazi occupied Tarnow, where at least until fall, 1942, you could always barter something for food. In the camps, the men were fed both poorly and inefficiently, and there was no other food available at any price.

Although there were over 7,000 prisoners, the dining hall could only accommodate forty men at a time. They ate in shifts from dirty plates with wooden spoons. "You got ten minutes to eat. Sometimes you finish your evening meal at two-three o'clock in the morning, and you stay awake for your breakfast if it's your turn to be first. You got your piece of bread and what they call soup but I call it dirty water." Shmuel's mouth twists as he remembers that odious liquid. "If you find sometimes the skin of a potato you're just lucky. A few grains of barley. Then we worked for twelve hours!"

The bread was like chalk. It crumbled. "The bread is nothing and the soup is nothing. You can last for one year. And then you're finished." The minimum ration was 400 grams of bread a day. If a worker exceeded his quota, he received 650 grams of bread with some kasha. "Two spoons of kasha!" Shmuel repeated the words to himself as if he could barely grasp their meaning. A worker who produced far in excess of his quota received double rations, 900 grams of bread, more kasha, "and sometimes you get something else, according what they send, some rotten meat. What's wrong for them is good for us!"

The prisoners' primitive clothing was rapidly reduced to filthy rags. Even so they were precious. You slept in your clothes so no one would steal them. The camp swarmed with vermin, mosquitoes, lice and bedbugs. "Those bites make you swell up. If you get five bites, you look like the hunchback of Notre Dame."

One hundred-and-twenty men slept in a small room, "on pallets, on shelves, four beds with thirty people in them. In the middle was a stove. You weren't allowed to use that." In a lumber camp the men weren't allowed to burn branches to keep themselves warm! Shmuel offered us another example of the camp's perverse disregard for the welfare of the inmates: the pallets were built of unfinished planks with the round, rough, bark-covered side up. There was no comfortable way to lie on them. "Thirty people lying like sardines. If one turns over, everybody has to." Shmuel's own story caught him off guard. He shifted uncomfortably in his seat. "It's very hard to tell you. Thirty to thirty-five years have passed. If you talk about it now, it sounds to me like a story from the Thousand and One Nights."

Even in the camp there was some relief. One room was heated. You could hang your clothes there to dry—an error, in Shmuel's opinion, because they picked up lice. But "if you get free, you got the right to go in that room, a warm place, and lie on the floor. It was an earth floor. That was—*uch*," Shmuel lets out an exquisite Yiddish sigh, "luxury."

Smoking was Shmuel's main pleasure. One day he was offered the opportunity of earning an extra roll every day for supervising a special lumbering operation. He agreed readily. It was a good deal. Not only would he get the extra food, hut he would also be "an advisor." He wouldn't have to exert himself too much. "Do you think I ever tasted that roll?" Shmuel never did and not because the camp authorities reneged on their agreement. Every day Shmuel traded away his roll for two rations of coarse tobacco. "What is a roll? But if you got two boxes of tobacco, you can smoke all day! Some of the soldiers weren't bad. They give you some pieces of newspaper to roll cigarettes." When they had no tobacco, the prisoners dried leaves and smoked them. They also received loose black tea every other day. Instead of brewing tea, they would smoke it. "It knocks you out." Shmuel smiled to himself, remembering that pleasure.

Packages from relatives sometimes reached the prisoners. Unaccountably Shmuel once received a huge can of lard in the mail. "It was worth a fortune!"

He tried smearing it on some bread and eating it, but it made him vomit. Was it spoiled? "No, but I couldn't eat that." The camp food wasn't kosher, of course, but Shmuel could stomach it. Pure lard was another story. He traded it away.

"There was a law in the camps," Shmuel told us. "You got to have a bath every month." In one night over seven thousand people had to wash. First they sent the men to the barber for a haircut. "A haircut!" Shmuel snorts derisively. "It's with a machine. Though, you know, to the skin, and then from off your face they take as much as they can. There were maybe eighteen barbers, our people." It bothered Shmuel to be shorn with the same clippers as all the other men, spreading filth and vermin from head to head. One of the camp barbers had owned a barber shop in Tarnow, and Shmuel had been his customer there. Somehow Shmuel's barber had gotten all the way from Galicia to Siberia with a few of the tools of his trade. Shmuel made sure that his friend cut his hair with his private clipper. That way Shmuel stayed a little cleaner. He pursued even the smallest advantage in order to survive.

After being shaved, the men had to disinfect their clothes, but Shmuel took pains not to leave his clothes in the disinfectant room. If you did, they picked up three times as many lice as before. The warmth of the room attracted bugs. "Shocking!" said Shmuel, in his Yiddish-accented Australian manner.

The next stop of the routine was another absurdity. They gave the men wooden pails full of boiling water and one spoonful of soap. The water was too hot to use, and it wouldn't cool off in the ten or fifteen seconds they gave you to wash yourself. Shmuel found a way to keep as clean as possible under those conditions. He didn't try to wash his whole body. He washed his head, and he tried unsuccessfully to clean his hands. The timber left the men's hands caked with resin, and you would have had to use a knife to get it off properly. Shmuel showed us his hands as if they were still coated with sap. Why didn't the prisoners overpower the guards and escape? Shmuel dismissed the possibility. The camp was fenced, and guards stood watch in towers. They had orders to shoot anyone who approached them. The soldiers also had dogs. Besides, the camp was completely isolated. The only nearby settlements were villages of exiles, people working in Siberia under somewhat less stringent control. The camp was some 500 kilometers away from the nearest city, across the Siberian taiga, a vast evergreen forest interspersed with swamps.

A friend of Shmuel's planned to run away and wanted Shmuel to join him. "You got a map?" Shmuel asked, "Where will you go? You speak maybe five words of Russian. You'll be recognized and brought back right away." The friend said Shmuel was a fool for not taking the chance, but Shmuel didn't budge.

The man did try to escape. He was missed at the next roll call, asking for trouble for everybody in the camp. Twenty soldiers set out with ten dogs, "and the next day he is back. But how? His clothes were all in pieces, and his body was in pieces." The dogs attacked him, and then the guards had beaten him. He was thrown into 'carcer.' His fellow prisoners each contributed a part of their rations and they bribed a guard to let them bring him the food. He survived the punishment, but Shmuel isn't sure whether the man lived to be released.

Shmuel's story showed why escape did not appear to be an option. It also showed that the prisoners tried to help each other as much as conditions allowed. Shmuel remembered a young man who refused to eat the camp food because it wasn't kosher. He was thin, pale, maybe seventeen or eighteen years old, the grandson of a Hasidic rebbe. He still wore his black yeshiva clothes. "He had never held a tool in his life," Shmuel said. The men tried to keep him alive, arguing with him to make him eat the food. Shmuel slipped into Yiddish again recalling the incident. "You've got to keep the body alive,' he translated for us. "He disappeared later on," Shmuel remembered. "I don't know what happened to him."

There were no rabbis among the prisoners, although many of them were religious. Shmuel remembered one Hasid whom he overheard in the forest, complaining to God. Another time, "I don't know, it was a miracle. Somehow a man from Poland got a parcel, seven kilo of matzahs. Somebody sent it, and he got it. It came exactly the week of Pesah. He never used it by himself. He went from one to the other one with a *kezayis* (the minimum amount of matzah to keep the commandment of eating matzah on Pesah, equal to the weight of one olive) matzah, *tzu filen es iz Pesah,* to feel that it is Pesah. And he just gave away the whole lot. He left only a little for himself."

The men kept track of the Hebrew calendar. The 17th of Av was his father's *Yahrtzeit,* the anniversary of his death. Shmuel assembled nine other prisoners so he could say Kaddish, the mourner's prayer. His father had died "a natural death" in 1932. Shmuel also knew the dates of his mother's and daughter's deaths, but didn't say Kaddish for them in Siberia. The support Shmuel demanded of the men who assembled for him to say Kaddish was undoubtedly returned when they needed their *minyan* (a quorum of ten adult men).

Shmuel knew that he mustn't fall prey to depression. Sometimes at night the men began complaining and talking about the food they wanted to eat. What's the dish you miss the most? How did your mother make *kugel*? "What is a person talking about when he is hungry? I always interrupted. What is the use? You make things worse."

Shmuel continued: "When I was in the camp, horrible conditions. There is no ink in the words to describe it. Even if I sit here day by day, night by night and tell you exactly what is going on and on and on. You have to write a book from a few thousand pages. I learned something in the camp. That is my nature. When you are bitter and you show it, every minute you are sick. You're a goner. Finished."

Shmuel wouldn't allow his friends to depress each other by complaining. He told them: "sit down and I will sing a few songs." Apparently it helped. "Of course, I forgot about eating. It made things just fine. And they laughed." The songs he sang were Yiddish songs that Shmuel learned from Poland. "Theater songs, folk songs, or *chazanishe* (cantorial) things, *nigunim* (Hasidic melodies). We sit for two hours, and I sang. They listen, and after that they would come to me and say, '*Shmuel, du hast arrangegibt a naie chayim*'" You gave us new life. Shmuel simply wished them "*a gute nacht*"—a good night.

He sat back and sighed. "Ech. You have to walk to work every day about twelve or thirteen kilometers. In the summer it is warm. The winter is six or seven months. And then you got cold rain. You go out in the morning about five. It's raining. The soldiers are well-dressed for the rain. But us? After one half an hour you're wet through. It's raining all day. Then you go back. You come home it's like water in a washing machine. On the way I started singing. They said to me, 'Shmuel, how can you sing?' I sing by myself. Sometimes is coming a soldier, just a *mishiginer*. He raises his rifle and says, 'If you don't stop I will kill you.' So I stopped. Fifteen minutes later, I started again." Shmuel grinned at the memory of his resistance. Perhaps it gave him no practical advantage measurable in rolls or kasha like the status he had earned because of his experience in the lumber business. But it strengthened him and it gave pleasure and strength to his comrades.

The Communist soldiers in charge of the camp clearly could not have been expected to let the prisoners worship together publicly. But on Rosh Hashanah, 5704 (1943) the Jewish prisoners approached the Christian Poles and Ukrainians in the camp. "Not the Russian ones, because if they know anything, they will never admit they are religious." The Jews said, "We'll make with you a package. If you don't go out and work on Rosh Hashanah, we won't go out on Christmas." The Christians agreed.

"Listen," Shmuel explained. "It's a few thousand people. What can you do? They told the soldiers, go ahead. Shoot. We will not work." The camp authorities gave in and made a bargain with the inmates. They were entitled to a day off every month. Rosh Hashanah would be exchanged for that day.

"One Jew, I remember him very well. How they overlooked it, I don't know. The soldier who searched him had no idea what it is. He got a *tallis* (a prayer shawl). That man *davened*, and we *davened*. And we *davened* with a lot of *kavanah* (fervor). Then the Russians arrested the *chazzan* (cantor)."

"We went back to the *minahel*—(Shmuel uses the Hebrew word for director/manager to indicate the camp commander). Listen, do you want a revolt? If you don't let him out, we are not going to work. You can't do nothing. In Germany they would have just machine-gunned everyone. But in Russia the *minahel* has to fill a quota. He is in trouble." Shmuel only re- members two occasions when prisoners were shot, and that was for trying to escape. The camp authorities released the cantor and the Jews finished their New Year's prayers.

During the first year and a half it appeared that one could survive the camps. As oppressive and harsh as the regime was, it still left room for maneuver. However, one night in the spring of 1944, the prisoners were awakened by the noise of trucks and soldiers. A convoy had arrived. They made all the prisoners dress and assemble outside with their belongings, "a few *shmattas* (rags) that's all." They selected some people for a new camp, Shmuel among them. By truck it would have been a week's trip over the rugged Siberian roads, but the prisoners had to march for three and a half weeks. They lived on bread and water during the march. At night they had no blankets. They built a fire and lay with their heads on logs. First their backs would be freezing and their bellies roasting hot. Then they turned over, shifting from side to side all night long. Like a barbecue," Shmuel laughed.

The second camp was dilapidated. The buildings were in disrepair. The roofs had rotted through and leaked. The men had to work in the forest all day, and at night they had to make their quarters habitable. Shmuel thought they might have managed when they were first sent to the camps, but they already were weak from a year and a half of forced labor and poor rations, as well as the long march through the taiga. The prisoners lost all hope of survival.

Shmuel's original sentence was for five years. It was extended to eight. "I was a hooligan," he explained. He never expected to live to the end of his term. Prisoners were dying, seventy or eighty every day. Shmuel's camp originally held over 7,000 men. About 1,700 survived to be released in 1945. "If you get, say, a cold, finished. Or something in your lungs, finished. You die like that." Shmuel snapped his fingers. "There was no doctor, no medicine, nothing."

At that point Shmuel envisaged no future whatsoever. "How can you think about building somewhere a place in your mind, but you are in a camp? You are just nothing, a piece of meat, a stinking piece of meat, a *shtinkindike shtik flaish*. Even then, although with no hope of survival, Shmuel wanted to stay alive. What was Shmuel going to survive for?

Shmuel said that then he didn't know that Jewish Tarnow had been utterly destroyed. Shmuel added a second reason: "I wanted to see what will be after that. I wanted to see what will be after that *gehennom*, (hell). But it was only a wish. To say the truth. Nobody got a chance to get home. It's impossible to survive in a camp." They only made it because of an agreement between the USSR and the Polish government in London. "That was the only miracle that happened." Traditionally we are taught that miracles come from God. But not for Shmuel. For him, as he often repeated "miracles come from yourself."

And Shmuel had a story of what was almost a miracle. "I never told you that one day I took a big rope and wanted to hang myself to death." It was in the second camp, where the conditions were hopeless. After a bitter day of labor in the forest, the prisoners were marched twelve or thirteen kilometers back to their camp. Halfway there a freezing rain caught them. They were soaked through in short order. "You can't *shlep* your feet. Like a horse that's ready to die. We came back and there's nothing to eat, not even soup, that dirty hot water. You lie down and your clothes start *shvitzing*, sweating. It's dirty. It's impossible. You haven't got the strength to stand up. You can't see yourself. You see the next one and the next one and the next one. See how the people are lying. You think, how long? They'll die. They'll all die. It's impossible. Why suffer? Why not make an end to it?"

Shmuel continued: "I remember. It was maybe midnight. I was sitting in my place, not sleeping, crying, and thinking about the whole thing that's going on." Softly Shmuel continued in Yiddish, describing his thoughts as he got ready to hang himself. "How long can a person live like this? What for? And just at that moment is coming someone to the barracks. I know him, I met him again in

Italy after the war and he says, 'You know what? Good news.' I forgot what I had to do, what I wanted to do. I was the only one not sleeping. I asked him, 'What's the good news'? 'We got free tomorrow. We're not going to work.' Shmuel's voice gets louder again. "You know what that was? *Mashiach iz gekimen*! The Messiah has come! One day you don't have to work! And that was that, that was the break."

Shmuel never thought of committing suicide again, but there wasn't much left to him when he was released from the camp. He had weighed seventy-two kilos when he was sent there, a healthy weight for a short man like Shmuel. "I was strong," he said. He still has a strong frame; he looks solid. When he was released from Siberia, he weighed only thirty-six kilos.

He suffered from "How do you call it? Avitaminosis (vitamin deficiency)." The body was not strong enough to take it." He looked down at his trunk with distaste. "Wherever you touched it, you got a hole. Running sores." He touched himself, as if it would happen again. He had been reduced to the absolute minimum human condition, only half a step above death. He had no material possessions at all. He barely possessed his own body.

The prisoners were released in order to join the Polish army in exile, the Andersarmee. "When I came to the army, I was like a skeleton," Shmuel said. He was in rags. "The main thing was to get rid of those *shmattas*. My shoes were just rags tied around my feet. I can't describe how, how…it was just….The worst beggar looks better than we were looking. Rags, *shmattas*, *shmutsig* (dirty). White people. Just white people." They took off all their clothes and burned them. They bathed and shaved. His voice swelled with remembered joy as he thinks of the new Polish uniforms they were issued: "I couldn't believe it. A life in normal clothes, normal clean clothes." The ones he had been wearing when he escaped from the ghetto had worn out, and the Russians had replaced them with a primitive uniform. "Believe it or not, the first shirt I got in the camp, I wear it nine months. Nine months." Shmuel told us that his father had put on a clean, starched white shirt every day. "Every day," Shmuel mused. "Nine months. You understand what that is? That is a story from a Thousand and One Nights. I don't believe it any more." One contingent was shipped to the Front. Shmuel was too weak to go with them. Another group was sent off for more forced labor in a quarry, a sure sentence of death for a man in his condition. Luckily Shmuel knew one of the sergeants and got an office job.

While he was in the army he sang Polish hymns during church services. "They knew I was Jewish, but I was the only one that knows those songs." He didn't stay in the army long. He knew he couldn't evade forced labor forever. So he stole a bunch of documents and deserted under an assumed identity.

He was cast adrift in Soviet Central Asia, Uzbekistan, a legendary region on the ancient caravan route between China and the West: Bukhara, Samarkand, and Tashkent. For him it was just the USSR, a country that had done him cruel injustice but that was at war with enemies even more implacable and dangerous. At that point Shmuel had no plans or expectations, nothing to build on, nowhere to go. He made his way to Bukhara. A typhus epidemic was raging there. He caught the disease and was brought to the overcrowded hospital. "A few hundred people are lying in the courtyard, just on straw mattresses. There is no room, no beds, nothing. Just luckily an old man, a Russian, died, passed away. Lucky for me, and lucky for the man also. He was suffering."

It just happened that the doctor in charge of the hospital was a Jew from Tarnow. The doctor's brother had been active in Hashomer Hatzair movement with Shmuel's younger brother. The doctor recognized Shmuel and saved his life. "They took me, and they carried me over all the people who were lying there and they took me to a bed. That was one in a million!" The next day Shmuel fell unconscious. For twelve days he was fed intravenously. "The doctor was doing anything he could to keep me alive."

"In the twelfth day, in the evening, I opened my eyes. The doctor said to me, 'you won the war the second time.'"

Now Shmuel had to recuperate and regain his strength. "Afterward you get an appetite. You are hungry like a *mishigge*. You want all day only to eat, eat, eat, and eat. So how can you get to eat? You haven't got no money. Nothing. The same thing that happened to me happened to a lot of people. They lie unconscious. They don't eat. They wake up very, very hungry." Shmuel's friend the doctor kept looking out for his interests. He instructed the male nurse who was working there, "you got spare from anything, the soup, bread, just give it to him.' I was eating all day, the next five-six days.

"I never stopped eating. Then he said to me, 'I can't keep you any longer. I have to; just to...' You can see what was going on." The doctor finally found a family to take care of Shmuel until he was better. "I couldn't even walk," he told us.

At last Shmuel did recover. He got work in a tiny mountain outpost and stayed there until he was repatriated. It was a coal-mining town, populated by Russian workers sent to the mines and a small group of Jewish refugees from Poland and Eastern Europe. The Jews made a point of distinguishing themselves from the Russian miners, whose thoughts, he claimed, were centered only on food and clothes. Shmuel and his friends held discussions about literature, the theater, and music.

Shmuel was no longer a *shtinkindike shtik flaish*, but life was still far from normal. "You're comparing in your mind, and it hits you. That is not what you expect." A few weeks before leaving Russia, Shmuel overheard two strangers talking in Yiddish in the street. They were discussing a job one of them had been offered. 'How much can you steal there?' asked his friend. "Because in Russia," Shmuel explained, "the salary is meaningless. What's important is what you can steal. For a normal life, this is just absurd."

Shmuel's stories about Siberia were utterly convincing. We reacted to them as we had to many other horror stories that we had heard or read about the Holocaust, but hearing them from Shmuel, and not about Germany but about Siberia, we reacted more intensely. We wondered whether he had told his family about those experiences. "How did your daughters react to your stories? Were they interested? How did they feel about your being a camp survivor?" Both girls found it hard to believe, he reported. How could anyone have survived? How could their father have suffered so much? Malka, currently an attorney in Melbourne, couldn't bear to listen. It pained her too much: she identified too closely, Shmuel reported.

Shmuel told us about the time Malka's teacher in Sunday school insulted her. Her teacher, an extremely religious native Australian, started talking about the camps, maintaining that the Jews had sinned, and that's why they had been sent to concentration camps. "Malka got white, and she stood up and said to her, 'If you want to give me a lesson about that, first have a talk with my father. Don't open your mouth to tell about what happened in the camps. What do you know about it?' Malka ran out of the classroom and went home by herself."

Shmuel continued, proud of his daughter: "When Malka came home, she was so upset she couldn't eat. I said, 'Don't take it so hard. It's over. Malka said she would hit the teacher if she started up again. The next day the teacher met Esther (Shmuel's wife) on the street. Esther said, 'She was upset because you were talking nonsense. You don't know what you're talking about.'"

Shmuel wanted to learn more about the reactions of the children of survivors. "I'm not the only one. You got thousands who are still alive. They ask questions." Against the background of Australian society, Shmuel's wartime experiences were anomalous. He was abnormal because of his great suffering and loss. In Israel, he was one of many survivors in a society committed to keeping the memory of the Holocaust alive. His background was woven into the fabric of Israeli society.

During some small talk at the close of one of our sessions, Shmuel mentioned a very religious watchmaker whose tiny shop is in a commercial hotel in downtown Jerusalem. The watchmaker was a wonderful old character, very warm and gentle, with a thick, long white beard and a broad smile. He always was dressed in a black suit, like a life-long Hasidic Jew.

"He was an officer in the Red Army," Shmuel told us. "He got medals." Shmuel had had a conversation with the watchmaker, throwing in a few Russian words. 'Where did you learn Russian?' 'In a camp.' What camp?'" Shmuel told him. The watchmaker said he had been in a nearby camp. During the war he had refused to do something, and they sent him to Siberia. "I was in Camp Seventeen. He was in Nineteen." In Melbourne you wouldn't run into a watch-maker who had first been a convinced communist and an officer in the Red Army, then a slave laborer in Siberia, and finally a pious Jew. In Jerusalem, if it isn't the watchmaker, then it's the locksmith or the pharmacist. Many people don't have to be informed about Shmuel's suffering, because they underwent similar experiences, or their parents did. A word suffices, the name of a camp, or a ghetto.

Shmuel felt that the war years formed a self-contained period in his life: set off from the rest and hardly connected to it. More than once he said that the time between 1939 and 1945 is equivalent to a whole lifespan, seventy normal years. Shmuel was thirty-seven years old when he went to Siberia. He still felt like a young man. He was old when he was released, although fewer than three years had passed.

Did Shmuel feel that his experience was beyond the grasp of those who never went through the same things? He took the idea and worked with it. "I saw a lot of suffering in Tarnow." He described a typical family in dire poverty, children shivering in rags during the Polish winters, and he said: "If you haven't got a feeling for that, then you are made of stone." But sympathy has its limits. "If you're hurt, I'm sorry. But it doesn't hurt me. I got only the feeling that you are hurt." His point was that until you experience the suffering yourself, you don't know what it's like.

Shmuel seemed to be groping for something quite complex. He remembered his work for the poor in Tarnow, and he realized that although he cared enough about their plight to help them, he never comprehended their suffering fully. Perhaps now that he had been as poor as any human could be and suffered as much as a person can suffer and survive, he knew the life of those poor Jews in Tarnow as he couldn't when he was a prosperous young businessman with a social conscience. We could sympathize with him, but we couldn't share it.

Shmuel pondered the issue further, and tried to address the question of reaction to his experience? "I'm not a man of hatred. What I want after the war, I didn't get till now. That after the experience, the suffering, that it would make them different people. But they haven't changed. They're worse. They learned how to kill more, to suffer more, how to punish people more. I'm disappointed. I'm very disappointed in people in general. I wanted people to be kind to each other after the war."

Did Shmuel's experiences give a special meaning to his life? Shmuel's answer was categorical: "No. A meaning you get only in normal life." For Shmuel, a normal life is life in Tarnow. "Every day the same, every week the same. With changes. But the main thing in my life was from 1940 till 1945. Those five years changed the way I thought one hundred percent. That was my life, what I experienced." In Israel, he found himself half living in his memories of the vanished world of Tarnow, the portion of his life that meant something. In 1939 he was the head of a family. In 1942 he had been reduced to a lonely individual. He was still a relatively healthy man then, but by 1944 he was just "a stinking piece of meat." Shmuel found significance and value mainly in what he lost, only partially in what he managed to regain.

Chapter Five

"How Far will it Go"

Shmuel often described himself as a rebel, and that became a private joke among us. One evening he was reminded of a wedding he attended in Tarnow before his own marriage. Shmuel hadn't been very eager to go to that particular wedding, but his mother insisted because the bride was related to her, part of an extremely religious branch of her family. At weddings like that, to this day, men and women sit separately, and they would never consider dancing with each other. The men dance on their side of the hall, and the women dance on the other side. Shmuel was sitting with a group of young men, getting more and more bored, until he finally bribed the band leader to play his kind of music, waltzes and popular songs. In a short time all the young people were dancing with each other. When the story got back to Shmuel's mother, she was aghast. "She asked me how I could do something like that." Shmuel's face broke out in a broad, mischievous grin. "You see, I was a real rebel!"

Not all rebellion was so good humored. Shmuel's younger brother, Naftali, joined the Hashomer Hatzair movement, a left-wing Zionist pioneering organization. He learned a trade, married, and left for Palestine in the early 1930s, at the age of eighteen. Shmuel didn't see him again until the 1970s, when he moved to Israel from Australia. Naftali's break with the family came early, and Shmuel's father seemed to have resigned himself to it. When his sister told her father that Naftali had stopped saying prayers in the morning and was only putting on his *tefillin* for a minute, the father's reaction was, "Better a minute than not at all." Naftali never told his father that he was a member of a secular largely anti-religious socialist movement, and his father never inquired too deeply into the differences among the various Zionist movements.

By the time Shmuel was a young man, after World War I, Tarnow was not short of rebels. Along with other socialist and social-democratic labor movements, the Bund was also active in Tarnow, representing not the dream of establishing a Jewish state in Palestine or an individual demonstration of defiance, but an ideology, which was meant to change the shape of Jewish society in Europe. The Bund held its meetings in a hall that shared a common wall with a large synagogue. Shmuel said that the Bund was careful never to hold a meeting or an activity when it would disturb services in the neighboring synagogue, and it was not uncommon for the same people to attend functions in both halls. Shmuel remembered going to a Bund meeting once and finding the daughter of a well known Rebbe there. She was sitting calmly among young men who openly violated the Sabbath. "I was surprised to see her there, but she didn't act surprised to see me." Her father never got wind of his daughter's heterodoxy. No one wanted to cause him pain or estrange them from each other. The daughter eventually became a Zionist and moved to Palestine. Shmuel has seen her at meetings of the Tarnow Landsmanshaft in Tel Aviv.

The orthodox parents of modernizing Jews in Tarnow seem to have been willing to overlook some of their children's waywardness as they slipped out of the tight grip of tradition, so long as the young people respected certain forms and avoided direct confrontations. Shmuel confided in us that he had once even attended a midnight Christmas mass in Tarnow. A Catholic school-fellow of his asked to go to High Holiday Services in the Great Synagogue, where Shmuel sang in the choir. Shmuel agreed and arranged to meet the boy in the early afternoon, so he could help him find an inconspicuous place in the balcony. It was a huge *shul*, and one boy more or less would never arouse attention. After that, in return, Shmuel asked his Catholic friend to bring him to Christmas mass when the time came. So at midnight on Christmas eve, Shmuel crept out of his house and went to the cathedral with his friend.

"I was never afraid of Polish people," Shmuel told us. He did what everyone else did at Church, kneeling down at the right times, and he drank in the music. "There was a choir of hundreds of children," he said, "I always loved music." Some time later, Shmuel asked his father whether he would believe it if Shmuel said he had gone to the cathedral on Christmas. No, it was too far-fetched an idea even to seem possible to his father, who would never so much as set foot in a church, let alone hear a Christmas mass.

Shmuel also used to go to parties with his gentile friends, Jews and Catholics danced with each other. He considered that kind of social mixing normal, although he didn't imagine it could lead to intermarriage. In a town where Jews attended Polish schools and spoke Polish well, barriers that had once seemed hermetically sealed had become quite permeable, up to a point.

During the first years of Polish independence, with the removal of the protection of the Austro-Hungarian Empire, there had been some pogroms in the Galician countryside. Half of the population of Tarnow was Jewish and the Jews were well organized and on the alert. One Friday in the early 1920s, a market day, "we have never seen how long we live so many peasants coming to the city, in the thousands. We know that something is going on. The peasants start not beating up, but robbing the stands in the market." In fifteen or twenty minutes the Jewish droshky drivers blocked one side of the market, and the teamsters blocked the other side with their wagons.

The teamsters were huge men. "When you see them sitting in the street, you just start shivering. You see big men, wide ones. From what? They were so poor they hardly ate a thing. But strong!" Shmuel described a teamster with five sons, all working together. They used to unload wagons full of leather, each bundle weighing over two hundred pounds. One of the sons, Ruda, stood out in Shmuel's memory. Before World War I, when he was only about seventeen years old, Ruda took a massive bundle of hides into the yard and danced a waltz with it to win a five zloty bet. "Five zlotys was a lot of money for him, two days salary."

The droshky drivers with their whips, the teamsters, who had armed themselves with clubs, and other strong young men waded into the market place and began beating the peasants. "Then it's finished. Tarnow was just famous for that. They know they just haven't got a chance." Polish students who molested Jewish families strolling through the public garden one *Shabbos* received similar treatment. "We beat them up and sent them home. No more. That was once. On Saturday, in the afternoon, the garden is ours!"

The more traditional Jews of Tarnow were hardly aware of the inroads of modernization until they forced themselves upon their attention. Shmuel remembers when the first automobile appeared on the streets of the town. A nobleman who owned four or five villages in the vicinity bought a roadster, and when he drove it into Tarnow for the first time, "the whole city was in one place." Shmuel had already seen cars, so he could look on the commotion with amused complacency. The nobleman drove slowly, and people ran up to touch the car. Some Hasidim were afraid, thinking it was inhabited by "*richus*," spirits. "You know, in 'thirty-nine' (1939) there were houses where they still carried the water from a pump. People couldn't accept that water could come out of a pipe in the wall. The first time a plane flew over Tarnow, they ran to hide in holes. They were afraid of that black thing in the sky; they thought it would bring a *magayfa*" (a plague).

Shmuel's father accepted modern technology fearlessly. When the Braw family moved into a new apartment after World War I, it was a modern place with hot and cold running water. As soon as electricity was available, they had lights installed. "My father asked my sister to show him how it works, and she took him from room to room. She turned on all the lights. He stood and he said, 'It's Gan Eden'! (Paradise!). How did we live in darkness before?'" When asked how electricity changed his life, the main thing Shmuel remembered was that they no longer had to clean and fill the smelly lamps.

Shmuel's married older sister lived in Krakow, which was much larger, more urban and modern than Tarnow. One day her father came on a visit, and she showed him her new gas stove. He was very impressed: "A wonder." But then he said that he hoped it would never come to Tarnow, where it would cut into his coal business.

A practical man, Shmuel's father spoke perfect Polish but never learned to read or write that language. At his son's insistence, he did learn to sign his name. Although he could, of course, read and write Yiddish with no difficulty, he chose not to read the various publications then in circulation in Poland.

"One day I showed him some newspaper in Yiddish. 'Read this!' And he said, 'What can I do with that? I can't change it. Can I change it? No!' 'All right, don't bother.'" Shmuel's mother read little more than devotional writings in Yiddish, *Tsena u'Reeyna*, the woman's prayer book but never novels, papers, or magazines. "She wasn't interested." Shmuel, on the other hand, used to frequent the local reading room, which received Yiddish periodicals from all over the world.

He also used to go to the movies, silent films by Jewish directors and actors, with captions in Yiddish. One day in the 1930s quite a while after his father had died, Shmuel persuaded his mother to go to the movies with him. On a Saturday night, after Havdalah, he took his mother downtown to the movie house. At the very door of the theater she balked. "I've been all my life without seeing a movie," she said, and she made her son take her home.

Religious observance was the force that guided Shmuel's father, not small-minded fear of new things. Shmuel remembered one Friday afternoon when no store in the Jewish part of Tarnow had coal except his own. He was married by then, managing the store by himself It. was winter, the store was mobbed, and closing time grew nearer and nearer to the Sabbath. Shmuel couldn't clear the store. People needed coal badly, and he didn't want to turn them away to face a freezing night with no fuel. Finally, just before sunset, his father appeared. "Jews," he said, "You have only ten minutes to light the Sabbath candles," but still they wouldn't leave the store. He himself went home to greet the Sabbath. At last Shmuel managed to close up, but barely before the beginning of the Sabbath, and it was likely that many of his customers would violate the Sabbath using the coal they had just bought from him. Shmuel's father was angry with him. He asked him, with resignation, "How far will it go? How far will it go?" For the rest of that Sabbath, he didn't talk with his son, the traditional Hasidic silent treatment.

Shmuel's father asked him the same question on another occasion. An important business letter arrived one Saturday morning, dealing with a matter that was worth thousands of zlotys to Shmuel. He couldn't resist opening and reading it, which you're not supposed to do on the Sabbath. His father noticed the torn envelope and asked who had opened it. "I couldn't say it was my mother, she didn't know how to read."

On matters less important than violating the Sabbath, Shmuel's father let him go his own way. One night, close to dawn, Shmuel met his father in the street. His father was on his way to the *mikvah*. the ritual bath. Shmuel was dressed in a tuxedo, wending his way home from a fancy dance event. They greeted each other, and Shmuel's father merely said he expected Shmuel to be at work on time: "The night is yours, but the day is mine" his father said. Shmuel didn't have time to change out of his dinner jacket and patent leather pumps. Still dressed for the dance, he rode off into the forest to oversee his workers as they loaded up the heavy carts with timber. When Shmuel got home from work in the afternoon, he took a hot bath. After that, he didn't feel too exhausted. His mother was concerned. She said to her husband, "Your sons are slipping away from you." He had to agree with her, but Shmuel said he took it with equanimity. Shmuel feels that his father would have liked to have been more modern, but he couldn't change. He was too rooted in the past. Nevertheless, he wasn't sorry to see his boys adopting new ways. When he saw Shmuel wearing a stylish cream-colored suit with white shoes, the latest men's fashion in Galicia, he said, "The Messiah has come! The dead are roaming about in their shrouds!"

Shmuel never had to fight hard against his father's authority. "Listen, it's funny" Shmuel would say, "When my father didn't like something, he just went away, and he never touched it again." Shmuel reports that his father said to himself, 'The world has changed. I can't change myself, but my sons have changed. What can I do? Nothing.' Shmuel had no regrets. Without rebelling, Shmuel detached himself from the network of constraints that tied his father into the old ways. Many Jews left those constraints physically: they went to America or any other country that would take them, and some, like Shmuel's younger brother, Naftali, went to Palestine. Other Jews departed ideologically, becoming socialists, communists, or simply modern, western-educated professionals. Shmuel freed himself without any ideological guidelines for his actions, by beginning to behave in a way that distinguished him from the extremely religious Jews of his father's sort. He was not the lonely yeshiva *bocher* (a student in a traditional religious school) one reads about in Yiddish novels, studying enlightened philosophy and other heterodox works on the sly, instead of tractates of the Talmud. Social pressure in the Hasidic circles of Tarnow was already too weak to suppress modernity. Shmuel's father asked of his sons only that they not embarrass him, and that gave them a surprising amount of latitude.

Shmuel never fails to speak of his father with veneration, for he embodied many of the values that Shmuel now misses in Jewish life: warm mutual support, unstinting charity, and spontaneous hospitality. "In Poland it was impossible to leave a Jew on *Shabbos* without a place to eat. That was Jewish life. Sometimes I was mad," Shmuel told us. "My father would go to the *bes midresh* (the study hall) to look for some *shnorrers*, (beggars or poor persons), one, two, or three. My mother expected one or two for sure, travelers or *shnorrers*."

Like his father, Shmuel was sent to a *Cheder*, a traditional Jewish elementary school. Shmuel remembers the *Cheder* as a dark, dirty, crowded, chaotic, and noisy place, where he was unhappy. At first he went uncomplainingly. "My father would lose a per cent of his prestige if they know I am going to a *goyishe* school." Nevertheless, Shmuel somehow managed to get sent to the state elementary school, where he was taught Polish in mixed classes: boys and girls, Jews and gentiles, together. His father let him have his way, up to a point. Shmuel continued attending a *Cheder* after school, and he wasn't allowed to attend the public school on the Sabbath.

World War I seems to have loosened the family's hold over Shmuel. The family fled from Tarnow to Budapest at the outbreak of the War and lived as refugees for four years. They managed well enough, never lacking for food or shelter, but Shmuel didn't attend school regularly. "My older brother started working, but I just ran around." When they returned to Tarnow, Shmuel was a lad of fourteen, too old to be shoved back into traditional Jewish schools.

He told us he would have liked to study at the Gymnasium, but there were informal and severe limitations on the number of Jewish students, and very few Jews even attempted to gain admission there Another alternative was the Real Gymnasium, a less prestigious, technical high school. Shmuel said he would have liked to study there, but his father wouldn't allow it, because he would have had to attend on Saturdays. Shmuel ended up attending a commercial night school for three years. Then for one year, he attended a school run by a well known Jewish educator: "You get a certificate from that school, and it's like you got a degree from the university."

As an adolescent, Shmuel began working, not in his father's business, but for his father's friend, a dry goods merchant. Shmuel likes to think of himself as someone who has worked hard all his life. Holding a job gave Shmuel independence. He said he was an industrious and responsible worker from the start. When a competitor of his father's friend offered Shmuel double his salary, he accepted. The first employer protested to Shmuel's father, who refused to interfere. It was Shmuel's prerogative.

Across the hall from Shmuel's family lived the Szabner Rebbe, a Hasidic Rabbi, and his father's spiritual leader. Asked directly about the Szabner, Shmuel would speak with respect and honor. Yet from time to time he let slip that it made him uncomfortable to have the Rebbe so close at hand. Shmuel was always careful to wear a hat even outside of his house as a sign of piety, a head covering that was the norm among observant Jews in Tarnow. "I didn't want to be a *shagitz*," a non-Jew. "I respected him (the Szabner Rebbe) one hundred per cent. You have to respect him. I would do anything for him. He was a holy man." However, like others of his generation, when Shmuel got a reasonable distance from the house, he would take off his hat and put it into his pocket. The times were changing.

Although he remained religiously observant, Shmuel left his father's milieu. Instead of his father's small synagogue ("just a normal *shtibl*—no rabbi, a *shammis* (sexton, caretaker), forty-fifty people"). Shmuel sang in the choir of the Great Synagogue. Every day during winter Shmuel's father got up before dawn. First he brought coal to the house of study, where he made a fire for the students and put water on to boil for their tea. Then he went to the *mikvah*. "All his life, till he was sick and he couldn't move he had the same routine."

Shmuel the rebel didn't always accompany his father to the *mikvah*. Shmuel went "three times a week or so. My father never forced me. He asked me in the evening. After I finished working I went off with *chaverim*, you know, friends, to coffee houses, to the pictures, everywhere. And he asked me always before I went out, 'You go tomorrow to the *mikvah*?' I said yes, I wouldn't say no." Shmuel was respectful of his father but was a practical man as well so he only went when the *mikvah* water was fresh. It was his respect for his father and not the religious injunctions that guided his behavior.

While he was still an adolescent in Tarnow, Shmuel developed a taste for traveling. Twice a year he went hiking in Czechoslovakia with a group of his Tarnow friends, under the leadership of someone older, whom Shmuel described as a wild man. They were members of a Polish-Czechoslovakian friendship club; therefore they didn't need visas to cross the border. Theoretically they were limited to the area within fifty kilometers of the Polish border, "but the Czechs didn't care." Paradoxically, although Czechoslovakia was a much richer country than Poland, far more industrially developed, goods were cheaper. "Poland was behind Czechoslovakia five hundred years. Everything they made in Czecho- slovakia was perfect." But a pair of shoes that would cost eighteen or twenty zlotys in Poland would sell for only one zloty in Czechoslovakia. "We came like beggars, without clothes, in old shoes, with empty cases." Shmuel and his friends returned from their hikes in the Carpathians with their suitcases bulging.

Shmuel liked the Czech people too. "They wouldn't take money for food. There were fruit trees planted along the road. You can take and eat how much you like. You come to a village and say you want to buy milk, they say, 'We don't sell milk.' They would give it away. They would say, 'You're hungry? So sit down'" They ate black bread, butter and cheese, and they slept in barns.

What language did Shmuel use to speak to them?

"We spoke some German, some Yiddish, and we learned some Czech, it's close to Polish. When you're young, you pick up quick." Shmuel thought of all the places he had visited and remembered what his father had told him: "You'll die traveling somewhere, not in bed."

The most religious Jewish boys from Tarnow avoided military service in one way or another According to Shmuel, most of them were too skinny and weak to be drafted If you were the sole supporter of your family, you were exempt, and there were always officials who were ready to take a bribe and let them off. However, Shmuel made no effort to avoid the army. He was strong and healthy, not the sole supporter of his family, and, perhaps, glad to be taken one step further out of orthodox society toward independence. He happened to know someone in the conscription office, a Catholic friend from school, who arranged to have Shmuel stationed in Tarnow. It doesn't sound as if Shmuel suffered very much as a young conscript in the Polish army.

After his release, Shmuel took a job in Krakow as a traveling salesman for a haberdashery manufacturer, a perfect job for him. We were surprised he didn't go right into his father's flourishing lumber and coal business, but Shmuel said, "I never liked my father's business." He knew that "first thing, the business was dirty. Every day you come home it sometimes takes you half an hour, three quarters of an hour to clean up, and you never get all that dirt off. Number two, I don't like how business is going on. I'm not one hundred percent a businessman. I am a good businessman, but it sometimes—I mean, you make in the business profit, you have to make a living, you have to pay tax, you have to pay everything but, in my opinion, business is always a swindle." Selling on a commission, not hiding costs or squeezing people, struck Shmuel as a less devious way of making a living.

The job in Krakow paid well. Shmuel loved traveling, and it was stimulating to live in a larger, more sophisticated city than Tarnow. The Jews of Krakow were more modern: "In Tarnow, ninety-nine percent of the Jews were speaking Yiddish. In Krakow, ninety-nine percent was speaking Polish. You see the difference?" They were Jews like Shmuel, who had gone to Polish schools, served in the Polish army, and who were used to social contact with Catholics. They no longer walled themselves into their own impenetrable society.

Toward the end of the 1920s, Shmuel had an opportunity to move to Berlin. His sister had married a German cousin and moved there from Tarnow. Now her husband had become too ill to run his business; he had served in the trenches during World War I, and poison gas had ruined his lungs. Shmuel came to help his sister keep the business going. He enjoyed Berlin, "It was a beautiful life," Shmuel reported with exuberance. In his opinion, no city in the world today is as pleasant as Berlin was then. Of course, most of Shmuel's friends in Berlin were other Polish Jews who migrated there. He said that the German Jews were very nice, but "very funny in a way," adapting the old assimilationist slogan: "They were a German in the street, but a Jew at home. The Polish Jew was always a Jew. He was a Jew in the street too." German Jews were formal and stiff, even at home, according to Shmuel, but not as stiff as the German non-Jews.

"Berlin was the best place of all to live," Shmuel insisted, and he lived well. But in the late 1920s he was summoned back to Tarnow by the Szabner Rebbe. Shmuel's father had developed kidney stones, and Shmuel was needed to help run the business. "I refused a few times. I didn't want to go." We were very surprised to hear that from Shmuel, since he had always expressed great fondness and commitment to Tarnow. Why not? "What go back to that stinking Poland, drunken every day, *shnorrers* in the streets?"

Finally Shmuel gave in to Szabner's pressure. "I never let my father down. He was to me just a good commander. I would do anything to please him, but I don't like the business."

Shmuel's oldest brother had already been active in the business. As their father became weaker and weaker, the sons took over more and more of the activity. Shmuel brought his father to a specialist in Berlin, who prescribed an operation, but the Szabner Rebbe was opposed, and Shmuel's father accepted his Rebbe's decision. "Jews don't go under the knife." None of his children would have asked a rebbe for a medical opinion.

Shmuel showed us a photograph taken of his father in Berlin. He is a dignified, intelligent looking man, dressed in a dark suit of modern cut with a tall, fez-shaped black hat, and his beard is neatly trimmed. Shmuel explained that the suit was specially tailored for him in Berlin. He had never before worn anything but traditional Hasidic garb: a long, black coat and a black, brimmed hat. Apparently he was willing to make a small gesture out of respect for the modernity of Berlin, although he refused the operation, and, when back in Tarnow, he seldom put the suit on again. He passed away in 1932 at the age of sixty-seven. "A normal death," Shmuel emphasized.

By the time of his father's death, Shmuel was fully bound to Tarnow again. He had married and had a daughter, Esther, and he and his brother were managing the business and prospering. The way Shmuel described it, his marriage sounded like an impulsive act, but it was actually the natural consequence of his decision to settle down after being summoned back to his father's side. He had taken a short trip to Vienna ("I always liked going places!" he reminded us) with a group of young Jewish people from Tarnow. Members of the group were housed with Viennese Jews; and at the end of his stay Shmuel proposed to the daughter of the family where he was put up. The girl neither accepted nor refused. She said she would think about it. They corresponded for a few months, and she finally decided to accept. She came to Tarnow where they were married. Her parents were originally from Tarnow, and she had relatives in the town, so it didn't take her long to fit in to Shmuel's Tarnow network.

It had not been a foregone conclusion that Shmuel would return to Tarnow and join the family business. His oldest brother had worked with his father from the start and his older sister also lived in Tarnow. She married a man from a nearby village, and Shmuel's father set her and her husband up in a business like his own. But each of Shmuel's two other sisters married cousins and moved away: one to Krakow, the other to Berlin. Naftali, Shmuel's younger brother, went to Palestine, and Yitzhak, who was six years older than Shmuel, ran away from home during the First World War to avoid military service, finally becoming prosperous in Berlin. Except for Naftali and Yitzhak, every one of the Braw children married either a relative or people with links to Tarnow. The family network extended from Vienna to Berlin, and its members could be counted on for assistance. Of course Tarnow itself was where the family ties were the most extensive and supportive.

Shmuel began to get involved with the Jewish community as was natural for a young businessman gradually assuming the responsibilities that went with prosperity. What were the religious divisions within Tarnow? Shmuel thought for a while, knowing our fondness for statistics, and then outlined his perception of the religious distribution among Jews in Tarnow and to show where he fit in:

There were first the *"mishiginnas"* by which he meant the extremely religious and mostly Hasidim who were about four out of ten Jews in Tarnow. Next were the *"frumme menshen"* or the very religious people like Shmuel's father. These were not the "fanatics" but traditionally observant Jews. They were about one-third of the Jewish population. And the people like Shmuel, who were of the younger generation, somewhat more casual in their observance, whom Shmuel characterized as "modern Orthodox Jews." They represented about twenty percent. The remainder, about ten percent were "non-religious" Jews. Shmuel insisted that even the people in the non-religious or secular category were very Jewish, not anti-religious, and not total strangers to the synagogue.

From the perspective of those whom Shmuel called *"mishiginna,"* he must have appeared almost nonreligious, just as from the point of view of the abjectly poor, Shmuel must have seemed like a very wealthy man. He, of course, thought of himself as religious as a sensible man can or ought to be, and he thought of his family as comfortably well-off, not extremely rich.

Compared to the Jewish manufacturers of Tarnow, the owners of the clothing factories, the candle factory, the movie houses, and the other big enterprises, Shmuel was just a small businessman. He joined an organization called *Yad Kharutzim* (Busy Hands), which represented the interests of men like himself in the internal politics of the Jewish community. That organization took it upon itself to fight for the rights of the Jewish poor, not within the community, but rather by addressing the Polish welfare officials. According to Shmuel, this was a significant development and departure from the past. Traditional Jewish organizations would have been afraid to provoke the gentiles. But the younger generation were feeling more comfortable with their Polishness, their language, education, and standing in the community.

The man in charge of the municipal welfare budget was not merely an anonymous Polish official. He was the town Bishop. Shmuel was sent by *Yad Kharutzim* to speak to the Bishop in behalf of the Jewish poor, because the funds available to the *Kehilla*, the official organization of the Jewish community, were insufficient. Month after month, Shmuel would come back to the Bishop with a list of Jews eligible for welfare, and he kept pressuring him to allocate funds for them. The Bishop knew Shmuel because he delivered coal and wood to various Church organizations, and he threatened to tell Shmuel's father that his son was a communist. Shmuel was not cowed, and he kept coming back, gradually increasing the number of Jews on the public welfare rolls. *Yad Kharutzim* had decided to take the Polish constitution at its word. If Jews were citizens with equal rights, then they should get their fair share of the government welfare budget.

The ideology of *Yad Kharutzim* was socialistic. We asked Shmuel why he supported a party that went against his personal interests as a businessman, a capitalist.

"First thing," Shmuel objected, "the word 'capitalist' is not the right word. Because we were well-off, but considering the other Jews in Poland, I mean from the business side, middle class today, true, we were well-off, but it's not the business by itself. It's the work. We worked very hard. Nobody was working for us. We were working by ourselves. Now, number two, in Poland, about twenty-five or thirty percent of the Jewish population, who were in that same situation, were called 'socialist.' We were not Marxists, but from the social life, from the Jews, we were more willing to be socialists. They were doing something for poor people. They cared about them, and that was the reason."

In trying to further clarify the organizational differences, Shmuel continued: "I gave money to the Zionists, but I wouldn't vote for them, because the only party who was doing something for the Jews in Tarnow was the socialists. I mean, just a minute, the Zionists were doing a good job, but, how to say, they weren't interested in local life. They only cared about the future, a thousand years from now, a dream. The real situation didn't interest them. Socialists were trying to help the people."

Shmuel told us several times that the Jews of Poland were second class citizens, and that the more traditional Jewish organizations were afraid to provoke the gentiles. He was not resigned to discrimination, and he was not afraid of the Poles. In his business he had some gentile competitors, and, in general, they got the Christian business and Jews got the Jewish business. Nevertheless, Shmuel didn't want to admit that anti-Semitism was a serious problem in Tarnow.

"A Jew would only buy from a Jew, but nobody thought about it." As for the gentile friends he made in school and kept through the 1930s, Shmuel told us he prefers not to think about what they might have done during the War. Until then, as Shmuel told it, there was a good deal of amicable give and take.

Tarnow boasted two large restaurants, a kosher restaurant run by Menasha Vachtel, and a Polish restaurant run by Adam Kaluch. "When Polish people had a hankering for Yiddishe fish, you know, gefilte fish, many came to Menasha Vachtel. But he couldn't make enough fish. So they went to Adam Kaluch and said, 'Why don't you make gefilte fish?' He said, 'I don't know how.' So he hired a Jewish woman to make it, and you got Yiddishe fish by Menashe Vachtel and Yiddishe fish by Kaluch, but that is foul-tasting." Shmuel and his friends used to say as a kind of a proverb, "If you want to eat fish, eat it by Vachtel, not by Kaluch," meaning, if you want the genuine article, you know where to go.

Shmuel told us other things about Tarnow that indicated a good bit of common ground between Jews and gentiles. If a Jew like Shmuel's father ever had some time on his hands, he would probably spend it in the synagogue, studying with his Rebbe or with his Rebbe's disciples. Not so Shmuel; before he was married, Shmuel used to take the train into Krakow on Thursday afternoons and go to concerts. He went to the theater often, both in Yiddish and Polish. On Sunday afternoons, he used to attend lectures in Tarnow, given in Polish by professors from the university in Krakow, lectures on general historical topics, or popularized science, given to a mixed audience of gentiles and Jews. The gentile world seemed to be gradually opening up before the Jews. There were Jewish doctors, lawyers, and engineers, and, despite the sometime virulence of the anti-Semitism about them, it appeared as if the Jews might be able to hold their own.

An incident that illustrates the situation of a Jew like Shmuel in Polish society is connected with a misfortune that befell his wife just after the birth of their daughter. Frieda Braw slipped on some ice and suffered a compound fracture of her leg which was improperly set at first in the Jewish hospital of Tarnow. She was laid up for months and months and the leg kept swelling and remained inflamed. Then Shmuel brought her to a Catholic hospital in Krakow for treatment. The doctor there taught him how to change her dressings himself, and Shmuel brought his wife home to Tarnow. For a long time the physician believed that her leg would have to be amputated. Finally, Shmuel followed the advice of a young Jewish orthopedist who was home on vacation in Tarnow. That treatment began to make the leg improve. However, one evening the wound seemed about to burst. Shmuel and a friend got up before dawn the next day and carried his wife to the train station and they took the earliest train to Krakow so they would be first in line at the hospital clinic. She was readmitted, and the head orthopedist assured Shmuel that she was nearly cured. A few days later, on a Friday afternoon, Shmuel brought some food to the hospital door for his wife, leaving it with the doorman as usual.

"And he said to me, 'let her take it by herself, I'm not your servant!'"

Shmuel imitated the gruff shout of the doorman.

"I thought 'a *chazerishe* (piggish) goy,' why does he have to talk to me like that?" The doorman locked the door, turned his back, and walked away.

"That's finished; I said to myself, 'What can I do, I will wait.' Then he comes again, he turns the key and opens the door wide. There she is, walking with a walking thing. 'I told you she would take it by herself. I'm not your servant anymore!' Next day I took her home. She got better, but she continued to limp."

Frieda Braw was a dressmaker, and she turned out expensive, stylish gowns that were much in demand among the wealthiest citizens of Tarnow. Frieda and Shmuel had a daughter Esther who they sent to a Polish elementary school rather than to a private Jewish school. They did speak Yiddish at home, partly because Mrs. Braw never learned to speak Polish well and partly on principle. Shmuel remembered once insisting that his daughter speak in Yiddish when she came home from school and wanted to continue in Polish. With Jewish friends her own age, she used Polish and Yiddish interchangeably. It did not sound as if Shmuel's household was the intensely Jewish environment in which he himself had grown up.

One sign of the change was in the religious atmosphere of Shmuel's household in Poland. Shmuel's wife never wore a *sheitel*, a wig to cover her hair. Shmuel's mother, by contrast, continued wearing one even after she began suffering from chronic headaches and the doctor suggested that she stop wearing it. In the late 1930s Shmuel's mother took a trip to Palestine, where, in addition to her rebellious youngest son, a religious daughter of hers had settled, as well as two of her granddaughters. Shmuel purposely sent her wig-boxes to the ship empty, so that his mother would finally follow her doctor's orders. He laughed slyly as he remembered the letter his mother had sent from Haifa, wondering who had stolen her wigs. Shmuel and the doctor proved to be right: she reported that her headaches ceased. But when she returned to Poland in August, 1939, she started wearing the wigs again. By then, of course, headaches were the least of a Jew's problems.

What did the future look like to Shmuel in the late 1930s? He was married, a father, a prosperous businessman, self-confident, and increasingly active in the Jewish community. Certainly he had no reason to expect that a Holocaust would engulf Tarnow and destroy almost every vestige of Jewish life there, all the buildings and all the Jewish people who lived in them. He certainly expected that despite poverty, discrimination, and other hardships, the Jews of Tarnow would continue to live there for centuries, as they had in the past despite all adversity. Most of its members probably thought that the Jewish community of Tarnow had a future, and that their own future was bound up with Tarnow.

Touching evidence of the expectations of the Jews of Tarnow can be found in the Memorial Volume published in Yiddish by the Association of Tarnow Jews after the war. It is a work of well over eight hundred pages, containing a long survey of the five hundred year history of the Jews in Tarnow, and many shorter articles about different aspects of Jewish life there. This volume is one of scores like it, all published after the Holocaust by survivors, commemorating their towns. Simply to go the library and read the names on the spines of these books is an overwhelming experience, as if the lives, energies and concerns of six million people have been compressed between the covers of books and arranged in alphabetical order on shelves. Those lost lives spill out of the volumes when you pick them up and open them, though of course they remain lost.

Certainly the life that is bound up in the Tarnow volume spilled out into our own lives as we handled Shmuel's copy of it. His brother had sent it to him from Israel to Australia, and Shmuel brought it back with him to Israel. In addition to the articles, the Tarnow Memorial Volume contains hundreds of photographs: prominent citizens of Tarnow, doctors, lawyers, engineers, and community functionaries as well as revered rabbis, the doctors and nurses of the Jewish Hospital of Tarnow, sports clubs, theater clubs, literary circles, Zionist summer encampments, Zeev Jabotinsky addressing a throng of Tarnow's citizens, socialist circles, and the board and students of the Safah Brurah School (Clear Language, a phrase from the traditional liturgy), a Hebrew gymnasium. The life one sees in those photographs is pluralist, modern, largely secular, and rather self-assured. The people in those pictures did not know that within a short time there would be nothing left of the institutions they were building, nothing except the memorial volume and the memories of people like Shmuel.

Religious life had not been eclipsed, of course. Among others, there is a photograph of a mob of Hasidim on the banks of the river for *tashlich*, a ceremony associated with the Jewish New Year. Shmuel explained to us that after World War I eighteen Hasidic Rebbes came to Tarnow from all the little towns in the surrounding area, and on the holidays their followers would gather by the thousands. The trams stopped, he said, because the streets were too jammed with Hasidim for them to push through.

"The street was black When you go out in the street, if you're, let's say, a religious Jew, but not a Hasid, they look at you in that way, that you're not welcome At *tashlich*, you can't even imagine. Two or three thousand Hasidim came just with the Shtutziner, sleeping on the floor in the *shtibl*, the small synagogue. The police would guard them on their way to the river."

"The *mikvah* was crowded like soup!" Shmuel said.

Shmuel feels as if he belongs in both kinds of photographs, with the secular activists, and with the Hasidim at *tashlich*. Although he did mention that non-Hasidic Jews were not made to feel welcome by the Hasidim, he would not admit that there was a barrier between the two kinds of Jews:

"They had the same soul" Shmuel insisted.

When we asked him whether he remained friendly with his most religious relatives, he was surprised at the question:

"What do you mean? In Tarnow, even Jews who weren't relatives had a warm feeling for each other."

"There was communication from one person to another person." In Shmuel's view, modernized Tarnow Jews had "changed their outside, but inside they were the same." Shmuel does not feel as if he ever left the old ways behind completely. "I accepted the way it is. I never think about changing it. The Jewish way, the main thing, I accepted, that is the way it should be. I wasn't as straight as my father, but my home in Poland was a religious home."

Yet it seemed that Shmuel had been on the verge of leaving everything behind on at least one occasion when he went to live in Berlin. What had his life there been like? What thoughts had he had? What plans for the future?

He was unwilling to scrutinize those two years of his youth. He mentioned going to a reform synagogue in Berlin once or twice, saying what went on there barely struck him as Jewish. There was no synagogue like that in Tarnow. The German Jews were stiff and cold and Shmuel had only a small corner of his family network to fall back on there. Yet he had been reluctant to return to Tarnow and join his father and brother in the lumber and coal business, a business that supported him well in a town he professed to love better than all others. We reminded him of what he had said about the Polish drunks and *shnorrers*, and he explained: "When I answered that question, I was not answering from the Jewish point of view, only from the life point of view. Poland was a thousand years behind Germany."

Berlin in the late 1920s represents a future that could have emerged for Shmuel and all the Jewish people in Poland. But memories of Berlin are now irrelevant to him. He had to make sense of what actually did happen. He showed no interest in exploring the jagged edges of the chasm that looms between himself and his native Tarnow. In Shmuel's mind, a bridge still arched over that chasm between Israel and those who once viewed Tarnow as home.

Chapter Six

"I Wasn't Lucky in Australia"

The distance between Shmuel's Jewish Tarnow and the Jewish State of Israel can neither be measured nor traversed. The bridge that Shmuel crossed during his lifetime now exists only in human memory. It disintegrated once Shmuel and the other survivors of the Holocaust had reached the other side, because no solid ground was left on the Tarnow end to hold it up. Shmuel's path from Tarnow to Jerusalem led, as we have seen, from German-occupied Poland to a Siberian labor camp. From there he returned to Tarnow, and when he realized he could not stay in his home town, he married Esther, a fellow refugee, and together they left for Italy, where they lived as displaced persons for a few years. Then they took a long detour to Australia.

The Jewish relief organizations would have sent Shmuel to Australia Third Class, but he managed to get a Second Class ticket by persuading a wealthy American cousin of his to pay the difference. Because of a complicated grudge harbored against that cousin, he decided not to settle in America. Just before the outbreak of the war, Shmuel's brother had arranged to go to America with his wife and twin sons They had visas, their household had been liquidated, their belongings were packed, and then the war broke out, leaving them stranded, and, ultimately, dead. A large shipment of personal belongings did arrive in America. Shmuel is convinced that they were very valuable things: sterling silver, fine china, and other luxurious household items. Shmuel's American cousin received the shipment and gave the things away or sold them. Shmuel thinks that she should have kept them for her surviving European relatives. Thus, in Shmuel's mind, any assistance he received from her was no more than the repayment of a debt. Angrily he remembered that all she had sent him was a package or two while he was in Siberia and a winter coat to his older brother.

In recalling this incident, Shmuel's mild, rather sweet manner became uncharacteristically heated. The bad blood represented by Ignatz's silverware had clearly polluted America in Shmuel's mind.

Shmuel knew next to nothing about Australia when he heard he had the opportunity of settling there. The attractions of the place seem to have been negative: Australia was not America, where Shmuel would have to depend on his wealthy cousin; it was not Poland ("I didn't want to stay with the Polish *chazerim* (pigs) any more"); and he had to leave Italy, where he would have liked to live on indefinitely. The only other alternative and the one that seemed the most natural was Israel (at the time still Mandatory Palestine).

Shmuel's youngest brother Naftali, had moved to Palestine in the late twenties. His sister Sarah, for whom he had worked in Berlin, had remarried after her first husband's death, settled in Haifa, and raised a family. He also had two nieces there, his oldest sister's daughters. Palestine was full of Polish Jews, Jews from Tarnow among them. By deciding to go to Australia, Shmuel was, in effect, deciding that he might never see any of his surviving relatives again. He claimed that the decisive factor in his choice was a letter from his older brother Ze'ev, who had been his partner in the lumber business. Ze'ev, a tall, strong blond man (he looked like his maternal grandfather) had found his way into General Anders' army after his family was killed in the Tarnow ghetto. Like many other Jewish soldiers in that army, including Menachem Begin, Ze'ev ended up in Palestine after the War. He wrote to Shmuel in Rome:

"After what you've been through, don't make life hard for yourself. Don't come to Palestine." He continued that there will likely be a war as the State of Israel was being established, and Shmuel had seen enough of wars and conflict already.

Shmuel took his brother's advice and postponed his move to Palestine for over a quarter of a century. The two men had always been very close to each other, despite the difference in their ages. In fact, in the middle 1950s, Ze'ev came to live with Shmuel and his family in Melbourne. They lived together for a while but it was a financial burden to add another person to care for in their household. Shortly after Ze'ev moved out on his own, he fell ill from lung cancer and died in Melbourne.

The Jewish community of Melbourne had arranged to sponsor a number of refugees from Europe, and Shmuel was put on their list, though he didn't know a soul in Australia. He remained in Italy as long as he could, but then he had to leave and was offered Melbourne, and he accepted:

"I went to Australia for good or for bad."

So, in 1949, at the age of forty three, with his infant daughter Rivka who was born in Italy, and a pregnant wife, not knowing a word of English, Shmuel embarked on the SS Roma for a new life in Australia.

The trip by sea from Leghorn to Melbourne is not short. The SS Roma was a luxury liner, and Shmuel remembered enjoying the fresh rolls they served on board. Other immigrants were on the ship, and there was a lot of printed matter about Australia, a land of opportunity. Shmuel had twenty-five dollars at the start of the trip, pocket money given him by the Joint Distribution Committee. Upon arrival in Melbourne he was already in debt to one of his fellow passengers. Traveling with a baby caused him expenses unforeseen by his sponsors.

How did Shmuel feel on the way? What was he planning to do? Was Shmuel gaining some of the optimism that he lost during the war and immediate post-war period?

"My permit was to Melbourne" was all that Shmuel would tell us, always evading a review of his own expectations, hopes and fears.

The boat docked, and all the immigrants were met by their sponsors except Shmuel and his family. He refused to leave the ship. It wasn't due to sail for three days, and he persuaded the captain to let him stay on board, where at least he had a cabin and three meals a day.

"I'm not so..." he began, but he didn't have to finish his sentence. His reluctance to step alone onto Australian soil with no money, no English, and no sponsor was self-explanatory. And unlike in Tarnow, Krakow, Berlin, Siberia, and Italy, Shmuel had no family or local networks to ease his adjustment to a new place.

"Why do you have to go out and stay in the street? *Mishigga* (are you crazy)!" he asked us rhetorically.

"After that what I get through, it was nothing special to me. I was sure that somebody would come for me. I got time, three days and three nights, so what's the hurry?"

The next day somebody did come. Shmuel's sponsor had been ill, which explained the mix-up. The man who met Shmuel and his family at the port spoke Yiddish. He was a member of the Bialystok Society, which had found sponsors for the Jewish refugees. Shmuel, Esther, and their baby daughter Rivka got in the man's car, and he drove them to the guest house of the Bialystok Society. Esther was upset. She wanted to know where she was going, what was in store for them, and the driver had no answers. Shmuel told her, "Relax. Enjoy the scenery. It's beautiful." Although it was clear that calm and relaxation were not the main feelings Shmuel had.

For ten days the Braws stayed in the Bialystok Society guest house. They took their meals at a kosher cafeteria nearby, and they waited for something to happen. Shmuel began to get more edgy, anxious to be out and doing, making some money, getting his family settled but his sponsor said, "Don't worry. Wait."

The Bialystok Society found a room for the Braws. They paid a month's rent in advance and gave Shmuel fifty pounds to tide him over. But still Shmuel had no job, and he was worried. His sponsor tried to reassure him. "They will come to you." Shmuel was not used to being taken care of by others or dependent on them.

There was a labor shortage in Australia at the time. Soon Shmuel got a job as a presser in a clothing factory. He was paid on a piece-work basis, and since he was quick and industrious, he soon was earning a fair amount of money, enough to live on and to begin buying the things they needed to keep house, from a tea-kettle on up. During the first years Esther didn't work. She had two babies to care for, Rivka the baby born in Italy, and Malka, their Australian-born daughter. Shmuel said he would have been ashamed to send his wife out to work. "What kind of man is that?"

Unlike his vivid stories about Tarnow and his experiences in Siberia, Shmuel was reticent about his life in Australia and how he felt about the place, but he was also not given to complaining, and he didn't dwell upon hardships of starting life in a strange country. Later, while discussing the quality of post-war Jewish life, he spoke of the emptiness of life in Australia from a Jewish point of view, and a more focused picture of his first years there emerged:

"In Melbourne, in a way my life was normal, but not in a Jewish way. Not what you're used to, what you want. Not only that your stomach is full and your body is healthy. You need the moral side too. You haven't got that. You can't get that. Malka was born in Melbourne, you know. For two years I saw her only on Friday in the evening and Saturday. When I left for work, she was asleep. I come home, she was also asleep. You know that on Saturday morning, when I told Esther I will take Malka to play with her, she starts crying. She doesn't want to go with me. She doesn't know me. She doesn't know her father! It's a stranger coming who wants to take her. You know what kind of feeling that is?"

"When you come home after twelve hours working, you want a rest. You have to get up at seven o'clock again. I was a robot. The Italians got for Australia four words: *Lavoro*, *mangiare*, *dormire*, and *finito*. You haven't got time. You are tired."

One reason Shmuel had to work so hard in the beginning was to pay for his apartment. After a short time the Braws had to leave the rooms that the Bialystok Society had found for them, and there were very few rooms to let in town.

"The Australians don't like to share their living quarters." Shmuel explained. "They like to shut themselves off behind their own hedges."

He learned of a rental apartment, for which he would have to put down 375 pounds key money, a fortune for Shmuel, although a low price for the house. He borrowed small sums from everyone he knew, five pounds here, ten pounds there. The day before he had to make payment he had raised 325 pounds, and he had run out of friends. Shmuel was despondent, and he is normally a cheerful man. In the factory a new worker asked, "What's the matter, you are not the same like you were a few days before." Shmuel didn't answer, but the new worker insisted on hearing his troubles. Finally, Shmuel explained that unless he came up with fifty pounds that day he would lose the new apartment. The young man took out his wallet and gave Shmuel the money. Shmuel's report of the loan was told with gratitude, but without emphasizing the Australians' generosity, how they trusted him, or that he was pleased to be living in an open, democratic society. Australia was a tough transition for Shmuel, especially in the beginning. He never felt it was his "home" or his community.

The Braws moved, and Shmuel started working as much as fourteen hours a day, six days a week, hefting a massive iron, to earn what he owed. He made a note of when his friends needed their money back, and he paid them off one by one, right on time. One of Shmuel's principles is to stay out of debt. Rather than buy a refrigerator on credit, he saved money bit by bit for eight years. When he had enough put aside, he brought Esther to the showroom, told her to pick out the one she liked best, and he paid cash. The clerk hardly knew what to do with his money, Shmuel told us, so seldom did a customer refuse credit. He is proud of his forbearance, and of that triumphant moment when he was able to put down cash for an appliance that would belong to him, not the bank.

We didn't think of asking him whether he had learned how to drive in Poland before the war. In any event, he soon figured out Australian society well enough to get a driver's license, which enabled him to get his next job: as a deliveryman. He slipped into that job by doing a favor for his friend, the owner of a Jewish bakery with customers in the outlying suburbs of Melbourne. At first he helped out on Fridays, which were the busiest days. He ended up working there full time. This job was an improvement over the one in the garment factory. The pay was better, the hours were shorter and it gave Shmuel a feeling of greater independence.

After a few years driving a delivery truck, Shmuel found an opportunity to open a grocery store. Another friend of his owned a shop which became vacant. Shmuel made an oral agreement with his friend concerning the rent. Then he fixed up the place and scraped together a bit of merchandise to stock it. At the start he had to put empty boxes on the shelves so they wouldn't look completely bare. After a year or two of hard work, cultivating his customers and cajoling his suppliers, the shop was doing well. Then his friend's wife, who was the actual owner of the shop, threw a monkey wrench in the works. She wanted to triple the rent and take a percentage of the profits on top of that. Shmuel was unable to resist her, because he had no written lease. He liquidated at a loss, and that was the end of his first business venture.

Next Shmuel negotiated the purchase of a delicatessen, but at the very last moment the sellers backed out, because Shmuel was a Jew. He says that was the first blatant anti-Semitism he encountered in Australia. Finally, he found another delicatessen and bought it. He, Esther and his two daughters, lived in an apartment above the shop, and for eight years they ran it. Unfortunately, urban renewal changed the character of the surrounding neighborhood, and Shmuel lost his clientèle. That was the end of his second business venture.

Then the Braws opened a vermicelli stall in an open market. With his outgoing personality, Shmuel soon attracted a lot of customers. He remembers especially the Turkish workers, who were suspicious of the other merchants, afraid of being short-changed. Shmuel would give them a pencil and paper and have them add up the bills themselves, and he would use their figures. The stand turned out to be a profitable little business, but Shmuel aroused the resentment of the other merchants in the market. They bribed a health inspector to find a spurious reason for closing Shmuel up. His third business failure.

Finally, during the last few years in Australia before his retirement, Shmuel and Esther sold costume jewelry, children's clothes, and sweaters (he called them "jumpers" in his Australian English) at the various open air markets in the Melbourne area. Sometimes they had to get up at three in the morning to be in the front of the line and get a good location, but they didn't have to work every day, and they made better money than they ever had. When he first got to Israel, Shmuel was thinking of importing a cheap line of Australian sweaters, but he thought it wouldn't pay.

Making a go of it in Australia forced Shmuel to compromise with strict Jewish orthodoxy that he knew growing up in Tarnow. In his first job he didn't have to work on the Sabbath because the factory was closed. But the Braws sent their daughters to an Anglican nursery school. The apartment they rented after coming up with 375 pounds key money was not in the Jewish part of Melbourne, where similar housing would have been much more costly. Their landlord was a Danish Christian, a bachelor, and a professional gardener. He lived in an adjoining apartment. For a small addition to the weekly rent, Shmuel's front yard received professional attention. When friends visited they couldn't believe their eyes:

"It's impossible. *Do lebt kain yid!* (A Jew couldn't be living there!)" Shmuel exclaimed.

Esther used to bring pieces of cake and an occasional meal to the landlord, and they grew quite friendly. The Dane decided to sell the place to Shmuel, partially to frustrate his heirs, who had visited Australia and betrayed greater interest in their uncle's worldly goods than in his well being and happiness. The papers were all drawn up, and the terms were particularly advantageous to Shmuel. On the very day they were to sign, the landlord went to town to do some window shopping and dropped dead. The property was auctioned off, and although the auctioneer connived in Shmuel's favor to let him get it at a good price, it cost him more than it would have if the gardener had lived.

The Dane's apartment was a reasonable distance from the Jewish neighborhood, but the apartment above the delicatessen was very far away, at least an hour's walk to a synagogue. There were no other Jews in the neighborhood, and, in fact, Shmuel says that his best friends were two Polish Catholics. To keep their clientèle, the Braws had to open their shop on

Saturdays. Esther used to stay there by herself and insist that Shmuel go to the synagogue. They sold non-kosher food, including Esther's own rabbit stew, which won the praises of everyone in the neighborhood, Shmuel told us with a half smile, and the customers loved the special taste. For a Jewish woman who has kept a kosher kitchen her whole life, except under the most extreme hardships, to cook a rabbit would be no less revolting than for the average American to sauté a cat. Upstairs, in their own kitchen, the Braws continued to prepare and eat only kosher food.

The Braws' daughters, Rivka and Mal, attended the Melbourne public schools. Being bright girls and fine students, they were accepted into a competitive girl's school of a very traditional English style. They wore uniforms and actively participated in school organizations. For a Jewish education, Shmuel and Esther sent their daughters to a Sunday school run by the Lubavitcher Hasidim and to their Beth Rivkah camp.

The girls have different characters, according to Shmuel. Rivka, the oldest, "is a good soldier," he told us, quoting the headmistress of the girls' school. Shmuel thinks it's significant that Rivka was born in Europe, whereas Malka "is a real Australian." Rivka grew up speaking Yiddish. The family already knew English a lot better when Mal started school. Rivka never challenged authority. Malka consistently stood up for her rights against arbitrary decisions and slights.

Malka was outspoken when their Jewish school teacher tried to tell her classmates that the victims of the Holocaust had been sinners. On another occasion, after the principal of the Lubavitch school invited the girls to his home for a holiday meal, Malka returned the invitation, and the rabbi refused. It was clearly because he suspected that the Braws' level of kashrut (observing Kosher dietary regulations) was intolerably different than his. Malka was offended. "Is that religion?" she asked her father. "I'm never going back there."

Telling of Malka's spunk obviously delighted Shmuel. She is a "rebel" too, after his own heart. On the other hand, he followed Rivka to Israel where the rest of his family lived and where he feels that he belongs. Rivka married and had children in Israel (Shmuel knew four of his grandchildren before he died). Mal remained Malvena, unmarried, an attorney working for the Australian government. She made aliya (immigrated) to Israel several years after Shmuel and Esther and worked in Israel for about five years. She lived with her parents in Israel but returned to live and work in Melbourne. Shmuel expressed great pride in Malka and her achievements. When he described her graduation from law school, with her gown and wig, his face glowed with enthusiasm. But, he said, "I can't get over that my girl is in Australia" meaning how much she has become part of Australian culture.

Something remains very puzzling to us about Shmuel's twenty-five years in Australia. Here is a man who could not be "more" Jewish, a native speaker of Yiddish, a product of the Hasidic society of Galicia, a survivor of the Holocaust. Why did such a man keep himself at a distance from the Jewish community he found in Melbourne? When asked directly, his answers were simple but we felt superficial: housing was scarce in the Jewish neighborhoods, the Jewish day schools were too expensive, business opportunities were limited in the Jewish neighborhoods, and the like. We could not avoid thinking that if Shmuel had wished to be more involved with the Jews of Melbourne, he could have overcome the difficulties he mentioned. In many ways he was successful, given his experience and his background and adjusting to a very foreign country. Our view is that Judaism in Melbourne seemed so thin and insipid to Shmuel, that he wanted no part of it. His image of Judaism was Tarnow in his young adulthood before the War and Melbourne was not Tarnow. Shmuel tried and failed to recreate his Jewish Tarnow in Melbourne. The absence of his extended family in Melbourne and their settlement in Israel was critical. Family was a powerful source of Shmuel's values and to his social and economic successes; his sense of failure in Australia reflected his being cut off from his family networks. Shmuel didn't feel materially deprived in Melbourne but was totally committed to providing for his family and children.

He told us that his reason for wishing to live after the Holocaust was the hope for recreating a Jewish life such as he had known it in Poland. He saw very quickly that there was no possibility of realizing his hope, not in Poland, not in the refugee camps in Italy, and certainly not in Australia. He used the analogy of a plant that has been uprooted and then placed in new soil.

"It doesn't work. The roots aren't in the soil."

Then he shifted to another metaphor which he tended to use: "It's acting, not real."

We thought that the subject of the Jewish holidays would lead Shmuel around to a different way of thinking about his Jewish life in Melbourne. The Passover Seder is always a high point in the life of a Jewish family. After the war, until he got to Australia, Shmuel attended group Seders with other refugees. They must have been unsatisfactory, certainly different from the

family Seders that he enjoyed in Tarnow. Yet when he finally got to conduct a
Seder by himself, for his own family, in his own house, Shmuel told us: "It was
nothing like in Tarnow. Since I left home, the holidays, the Seder, the *hagim*
(holidays), the *minhagim* (the customs and rituals), have not been anything like
it. Never. Not here in Israel. *Es hot nisht die kraft. Es is artistish gemacht* (It
doesn't have the style. It is artificial.). Why? I don't know."

We wondered if his wife Esther felt the same way.

"I never asked her." Shmuel was surprised at the question, and perhaps
surprised that he never shared his feelings. Then he put the question generally:
"Do Americans in Israel find Jewish life in Israel to be genuine, or to be
artificial, on a stage, a show in a theater?" For many, America was the show.
Shmuel cannot put himself in our place. And we understood over time, after
many hours of conversation, how difficult it was for us to put ourselves in his
place.

In Australia, he said with smile, there were some religious Jews who kept
'all' the holidays, including Christmas. We all chuckled. Again, this was a
radical experience for Shmuel.

He went on to tell us that arrangements were made in Jewish neighborhoods
in Australia to sell food that was kosher for Passover. One area of a supermarket
was set aside and marked off, and Passover goods were sold under the super-
vision of an observant Jew. So it was possible to make do there. Still, Shmuel
wondered, how kosher is it to keep Passover food in the same room as regular
food? In Tarnow such a thing would never have happened. Also, "why did the
Passover food cost more?" he asked rhetorically. He saw the rabbi takings bags
of sugar, the same sugar you got all year around, putting a special "Kosher for
Passover" stamp on it, and then raising the price five or ten percent "What kind
of a swindle is that?," he asked.

Why was Shmuel so offended? After all, he never claimed to be an
extremely pious man. He has always been a modern person.

"It does not have to do with religion; it has to do with *erlichkait*
(conscience) and some moral principles. If you represent something to be
something, then that's what it must be. The swindle hurts me more than
anything. All or nothing. I don't want a combination. You can't wear a
Shtraimel (a Hasidic fur hat) and a cream-colored suit. In Melbourne there was a
butcher with kosher for Pesach meat on one side of the store and pork on the
other. What kind of kosher is that? You just take the wrong knife by mistake,

and it's finished. Or you are, or you are not. That is the point. They weren't selling kosher food; they were selling *tsettelach* (labels).

"You didn't have that Jewish feeling in Melbourne, but you did in Tarnow: even though eighty percent didn't even understand the siddur (prayer book), they had a deeper religious, Jewish feeling." According to Shmuel, the Jews of Poland feared God, and they would have continued fearing God, maybe a little less intensely, but still more strongly than in Australia. There was real social pressure in Poland: "They wouldn't let you go another way." The Jews of Poland would never have stopped speaking Yiddish, "because there are things you can say in Yiddish that you just can't say in Polish or English."

Shmuel did not hold himself aloof from the Melbourne Jewish community. He was a member of a synagogue, and when the synagogue built a succah (a booth used on the Succoth holiday) he would sit in it with the others to perform the *mitzvah* (ritual) and say the blessing. He received the community newsletter, which was half in Yiddish, half in English. He laughed when he remembered it. It was mostly about who was getting married, who was having a Bar-mitzvah, who had children, and who passed away. No real news. He also participated in fund-raising drives for Israel.

He told us about an Arab Christian acquaintance of his who attended a United Israel Appeal rally in 1967, after the six day war. Shmuel proudly stated that the man left in tears to see so much charity being collected for Israel. "Jewish people are still generous," Shmuel admits, but after the crisis has passed, "It's as if nothing has happened. In normal life, people are not normal. See, just the opposite. When it's not normal life, they start to be normal." Normal, for Shmuel, is the way he wants to remember Tarnow, where Jews spontaneously offered assistance whenever a fellow Jew was in need.

Generally Shmuel tries to see things as they are. He is aware of the objective differences between Tarnow and Melbourne. Tarnow was a small city in a small area, half of whose inhabitants were Jews and whose ancestors had lived in Tarnow or the immediate vicinity for generations. Melbourne is a new sprawling city with more than two million inhabitants, very few of whom are Jews. Moreover, the Jews of Melbourne are largely recent arrivals. As Shmuel put it: "Melbourne is very big. You are not living compact with Jews." People who were otherwise fairly observant moved out to the suburbs and started driving their cars in on Saturday to go to religious services, for example. From a religious point of view, as Shmuel understood it, that is a serious breach in orthodoxy, and from a social point of view, that was a sign of the dilution of the Jewish community. For one reason or another, either to live over their delicatessen stores or to enjoy the graciousness of suburban living, Jews stopped making an effort to live near other Jews.

Unlike the Jews of Tarnow, who lived in staggering poverty, but who dedicated their lives to observing the Sabbath and enjoying it "the Jews of Melbourne got no *menucha* (tranquil restfulness)." In general, they built themselves up from nothing. "A lot of people were very lucky. Sixty percent was lucky. Fifteen percent was very lucky." Shmuel told us about a few fabulously successful Melbourne Jews, shaking his head in bemused disbelief at their good fortune. He betrayed no envy of them. Their frantic upward mobility was alien to him. He didn't approve of the way they brought up their children or their lifestyle and values.

Australian gentiles didn't spoil their children, he told us. They made them go to work, and they made them contribute to household expenses. But Jewish people gave their kids everything: clothes, stereo sets, and cars. Ruefully Shmuel remembered several bad accidents among spoiled Jewish adolescents whose parents had given them fancy cars as soon as they reached driving age. "The Jews in Australia. I understand very well. They only want to be rich and to be something. You know, 'I am something, I got the money.'"

Shmuel has a peculiarly sane attitude towards money. He said it wasn't until he reached Australia that he understood that money means power. Evidently he had not perceived himself as a powerful man in Poland, even though he had money. For Shmuel, money is nothing but a means of getting something else that you need.

"All my life, if I had money to buy something, I wouldn't refuse. If I didn't have the money, so I didn't buy. What's money good for? There are no pockets in the shrouds. Money is dead."

Once, while he was running the grocery store, his account was overdrawn, and the bank manager called him in to discuss the matter, Shmuel said to the manager: "What difference does twenty-five or fifty pounds make? You've got millions lying around here!" He made a sweeping gesture as if we were now sitting in the bank vault surrounded by piles of currency. Then he laughed, "He kicked me out of the office."

The Jews of Melbourne were tense because of their money fever. "They always got something on their minds. Another thing was gambling. The Jews in

Australia were big gamblers." But hadn't Shmuel told us about the gambling in Tarnow? Shmuel laughed: "In Tarnow, what did they have to gamble with? What horse races? Where? Sometimes, on Chanukah, on Purim, my father went to play dice with *haverim* (friends). That was all. Finish. In Australia the Jewish people are gambling on horses, on dogs, any kind. Mostly horses."

He told us an old Jewish joke, adapted to Australia. "Two Jewish businessmen meet on a Sunday morning in the lane behind their shops. Even though it was against the law to open on Sunday, Jews used to come in and do paper work, get the books in shape, catch up on inventory. They start talking. One of them asked the other, 'How did you do at the races yesterday?'"

"I picked three winners, three good horses. What about you?"

"I lost again, as usual. What's your secret?"

"Listen, I'll tell you. Every Saturday, before I go to the races, I go to the synagogue, pledge a contribution and when I am called up to the Torah, I make a special prayer for the horses."

A week later, the men meet again as they are leaving their shops, "Well," asked the first one, "How did it go?"

"I did just what you said, but I still lost."

"What synagogue do you go to?"

Here Shmuel gave us the name of one of the well-known synagogues that he didn't go to in Melbourne.

"No wonder," said the first man, "that synagogue only works for the dogs!"

A variant of that joke is probably told about Jews in every western nation in the world. It points right at the core of the confusion of values that made Shmuel feel marginal even to the marginality of Australian Jewish life. Shmuel summed up his more than a quarter century in Melbourne: "I wasn't lucky in Australia." It seemed that he simply was unwilling to give himself over to the frantic struggle to make a fortune. He is a skilled businessman but is not an entrepreneurial gambler.

Shmuel was also unwilling to fall back on the Jewish community for assistance, because help was offered with too much fanfare. Perhaps he could have borrowed money, started off better capitalized, and ended up richer, but he didn't want to provide an opportunity for some well known philanthropist to pat his own back in public. The attitude should be, according to Shmuel, "I want to help. What's to talk about?" Shmuel was satisfied with what he managed to earn with his own hard work, and he was proud to have been a working man all his life.

One heard a hint, though, of some bitterness when Shmuel talked about the girls. When they were in high school, they asked for charge cards in a large department store where all the other girls bought things. Shmuel arranged for the cards, but he warned the girls that he didn't have enough money to pay for anything that wasn't absolutely necessary. If they ever splurged or acted irresponsibly, he would close the account and return the merchandise. Shmuel is a generous man, and he hates to refuse anyone anything. Yet he also hates to see people emulate each other in conspicuous consumption. In a community where Jewish children were showered with material things, Rivka and Malka must have felt materially deprived.

Rivka was especially sensitive to the snobbishness of the Jewish community of Melbourne. Shmuel recalled that once a boy broke off with her when he found out that her father sold pasta in an open air market. Rivka was hurt, naturally enough. Certainly one reason she moved to Israel was to escape the materialistic snobbery of Melbourne. Malka, on the other hand, seems to have decided to beat the community at its own game, becoming an attorney and moving up in the world.

Intermarriage, which was virtually unthinkable in Tarnow, was not uncommon in Australia, and Shmuel's attitude seemed surprisingly tolerant. He admitted that he would be upset if Malka married a non-Jew, but he wouldn't go so far as to regard her as dead and sit *shiva* (in mourning) or say kaddish (the mourner's prayer) for her. He couldn't see how anyone could pretend that his child was dead. "Sure, I would be upset, but what can I do?"

He remembered the case of his friends, Jewish people, who lived next door to a Greek family. Their son married the neighbor's daughter, and both families were heartbroken. After the wedding, the children moved to a distant suburb, and the two sets of in-laws never even said good morning to each other. After some time, the Greek girl was accepted by her Jewish parents-in-law, although the Jewish boy was never accepted by her parents. "She's a wonderful girl," said Shmuel "Why shouldn't his parents be friendly with her? It's their son's wife."

When Shmuel mentioned non-Jews, they usually were fellow immigrants: Poles, Italians, Greeks, Turks, and his Danish landlord. As for the Anglo-Saxon Australians, they are a strange breed in Shmuel's opinion. They sequester themselves behind hedges and seldom say more than "Good morning, nice day, isn't it?" On the other hand, they are very informal and never use "Mister." They keep their Sabbath in an odd way, at least from a Jewish point of view: banning football, closing businesses, but working in their gardens and washing their cars They spend a lot of time in pubs, ordering five or six glasses of beer just before closing, lining them up on the bar, downing them one by one. Shmuel hated pubs in Melbourne. They were too noisy and they stunk of beer. He preferred to buy beer and drink it at home, and never went to pubs except when he had to buy someone a drink for business reasons.

He claimed to have encountered very little overt anti-Semitism. Shmuel was a "New Australian," and what hostility he did encounter was not specifically anti-Semitic, but rather xenophobic. Several times missionaries approached him, but conversion held no attractions for Shmuel. Being a Jew had undoubtedly brought him more than his fair share of tribulations, but was Christianity any better? "Why do I have to trade my shit for yours?" Shmuel asked, embarrassed that his coarse language should be heard by us and preserved by our tape recorder.

Rivka went to Israel first She won a scholarship to do graduate work at the Hebrew University. After a few years, Shmuel and Esther decided to follow her. Not that he was ever a Zionist, he protested, "I just wanted to come to Israel to live the last few years of my life." Shmuel's friends were surprised by his decision. How could he move to a country he'd never even seen after all those years in Australia, where life was so good. The Australian Jews who had visited Israel were particularly surprised that Shmuel had decided to live there. On balance, Shmuel is glad that he left Australia, although Israeli society is a bitter disappointment to him. He told us that he still hopes that his other daughter Malka will leave Australia. Except for her presence there, it would seem to Shmuel as if he had never really been in that country. He certainly has no nostalgic feelings for his life there.

During the twenty-five or so years he lived in Melbourne, Shmuel never took a trip out of the Melbourne area. He saw more of Italy in his three years there than he did of Australia. "You know, in the last five years, seventy-five, eighty percent I've forgotten about Melbourne." (His voice sounded mildly surprised) "I can't remember the names of the streets." Then, decisively, he added; "Now I am a Yerushalmi (a Jerusalemite)."

Chapter Seven

"They Dry Out"

"The first time I go to the Wall, I have to pinch myself. Meir Braw's son at the *Kotel* (the Western Wall, a remnant of the Temple period and a holy site in Jerusalem). It couldn't get through. I remember that my father had a picture of the *Kotel* on the wall in Tarnow. Frequently, I see him staring at that picture. What he was thinking? He never told me. And I don't ask him. I know it's a feeling you don't touch."

For centuries, religious Jews all over the world have hung pictures of the Western Wall of the Temple Mount on the eastern wall in their main living rooms. That is the closest to Jerusalem most Jews over the years ever came to the site of the holy temple. A Jew's spiritual compass is attracted to that pole. It is there that individual prayers would be recited when not in the synagogue. Whenever a twenty-first century Jew reaches the Wall, he can hardly help being flooded with the longings of generations and generations of his ancestors, who were unable to step forward and touch those massive stone blocks. One feels as if a centuries' old desire has been satisfied when one's fingers explore that hewn surface. It is a feeling you can't touch.

"I'm not a Zionist. Not today, and not in the 1930s. I'm a Jew. I want to see the Jews be a nation like the other nations." Except for religion, Shmuel's aliyah, his immigration to Israel, was not ideologically motivated, at least not directly. His older daughter, Rivka, was always active in a Zionist youth movement in Australia, and she moved to Israel before her parents. Like other young Jews living outside of Israel, in the Diaspora, who find that they don't fit into the society about them and focus their lives on a Jewish youth movement, Rivka became a youth leader and put more and more of her energy into Zionist activities. She was offered a scholarship by the Jewish community of Melbourne to study at the Hebrew University in Jerusalem; that was the natural and fortunate outcome of a process that had begun long before.

Anyone who knew Esther and Shmuel had to admire their courage, their cheerful good spirits, their warmth, and their enthusiasm for life. To have such parents and to carry on their mission of survival is no insignificant matter. Yet the operative values of the upwardly mobile Jewish community of Melbourne and the bland suburban ways of gentile Australia cannot encompass people like the Braws. Rivka smarted under the snobbish cuts administered by her fellow Jews. Once she reached Israel, she immediately began working on bringing her parents to live in Israel as well.

Shmuel had carried on a correspondence with his sister in Haifa, and, to a lesser extent, with his brother, nieces and cousins in Israel. Naturally he expected to move to Haifa, and he was disappointed when Rivka reported that the only available housing for new immigrants was in Jerusalem. The Jewish Agency, the organization responsible for the integration (they refer to it as "absorption") of new immigrants into Israeli society, was providing subsidized long-term rental housing for retired immigrants in Jerusalem and nowhere else. So Jerusalem is where Shmuel had to live, like it or not. Once he had lived in Israel for several years, Shmuel appreciated the difficulties Rivka had to surmount, pushing her request through the bureaucratic barricades, and he came to love Jerusalem.

He didn't say as much, but any objective consideration of his prospects in Australia, after retirement, must have seemed rather grim. Especially after Rivka left. What did he and Esther have to look forward to except lonely old age? In Israel, Shmuel could reasonably expect to be less lonely. And, in fact, he was not a lonely man, for he had many friends in similar circumstances: retired and of East European origins. So he could share conversations in Yiddish, compare the culinary varieties of East European foods, and complain about this and that in Israel. These are all positive signs of absorption.

In part, Shmuel was dissatisfied with life in Israel. One can't quite say that Israel did not come up to Shmuel's expectations. If he had had high expectations, he would have come to Israel in 1948, or he would have lived in Australia in constant yearning for the Jewish State. But, in fact, his decision to make aliyah came as a surprise to his Australian friends. Shmuel summed up his complaints about Israel in one sentence: "It's a beautiful country, but I don't like the Israelis." He had no Israeli hero, he said, and he rejected the proverbial definition of the Israeli as a Sabra, prickly on the outside but sweet within. "They are harsh all the way through" he told us. Israel had a bad effect on his relatives, too. "They dry out" he said with some bitterness and disappointment.

Once, Shmuel said that it had been more than a year and a half since he'd gone to Haifa to visit his sister and brother. We had expected that a warm and friendly man whose family had been wiped out in the European Holocaust would cherish his few surviving relatives like the apple of his eye–a brother whom he hadn't seen for several decades from the late 1920s to the 1970s, and a sister whom he hadn't seen since the middle 1930s! Yet, when one thinks about it objectively, and Shmuel was a very objective man, for all their being brothers and sisters, they had led separate lives. People change a lot in forty years, especially when they live through dramatic historical events. We know something about Shmuel's experiences in Poland, Russia and Australia. We can only imagine his family's experience in Palestine/Israel during the British Mandate, the Arab riots, the Second World War, the War of Israel Independence, the troubled years of the state's infancy and the wars in 1967 and 1973. Moreover, a language barrier had grown up between them. Shmuel never stopped using Yiddish, but his family had long since switched over to Hebrew, and Shmuel couldn't speak Hebrew fluently or comfortably.

Shmuel felt that his nieces and nephews neglected him and took him for granted; only getting in touch with him when they needed someplace to stay in Jerusalem. Except for his daughter and her family, the only relative he seemed to see frequently was an aged cousin who lived in an extremely religious neighborhood in Jerusalem. His cousin was very feeble, and Shmuel visited him regularly. He did call his sister in Haifa every couple of weeks, staying in touch, but his life in Israel turned out to be independent of his longstanding family ties to the country.

Like most people, Shmuel's opinions of the society he lived in were formed partially from personal experience and partially from newspapers, radio and television. For example, he believed that Israelis must learn to live on what they earn, a commonplace of public opinion where the national budget exceeds the gross national product. Israelis lacked discipline, he claimed, and they weren't willing to work.

"After a while, your rich uncle will get tired of giving you *shnorrer gelt* (beggar's money)." It upset Shmuel that everyone disparaged Israeli currency.

"They say the money is worthless, but they will cheat you for it, and it will still buy you something."

Once, a man overcharged Shmuel, selling him a glass of juice for three Israeli pounds instead of two. When Shmuel protested, the man said, "What's to you another pound? He thought I was a rich American Jew." Years afterwards the experience still rankled.

Israeli society was permeated with the same kind of materialistic emulation as Jewish society in Melbourne, Shmuel thought. Once, before his daughter moved to Kibbutz Ein Zurim, they went to stay with her in Arad, a small town south of Jerusalem and east of Beer Sheva. While they were there, they visited friends of his daughter's, people originally from England. The whole conversation revolved around the acquisition of furniture, the alteration of apartments, and borrowing money to finance these projects. "I sat there, and I listened. I didn't say anything the whole time. But when I got home, I told Rivka I didn't want to hear that she's borrowing money for things like that. If you haven't got the money, don't buy it." Israel was full of people spending money they don't have, Shmuel thought. He subscribed to the peculiar and widespread myth that the reparations paid to victims of the Holocaust by the West German government created that unhealthy economic climate. It is held that, before the reparations everyone was reasonably poor and lived in harmony. The reparations created inequality, aroused envy and ruptured the social fabric of the growing nation, undermining the work ethic above all, by making everyone want to get something for nothing. That is received opinion in Israel. and Shmuel accepted it as a reasonable explanation for what he saw about him.

Shmuel was a sharp-eyed observer, and he generally sought to support his opinions with personal experience. Waste offended him, especially waste in religious institutions. A woman he knew in Melbourne used to cook for a yeshiva (religious academy) there, and according to her, they wasted enough food to feed a dozen poor families. Shmuel was still appalled by her reports years later, and they reinforced his low opinion of the religious establishment. There was a small yeshiva up the road from Shmuel's Jerusalem apartment, and when he passed it, he said he often saw boxes of untouched food out with the rubbish. A yeshiva, supported by charity and public funds, shouldn't waste a penny. "Why do they have an Arab sweeping out the yard? The boys can't work a bit to keep the yeshiva tidy?" In Poland, only the very poorest took charity, and they didn't waste what they received. He didn't think yeshiva students should be supported without working.

In Poland, Shmuel contended, the Jews were second class citizens, the first to pay taxes and the last to receive any benefits from the government. "Ninety percent they haven't got any rights. Here in Israel the religious are the first ones to get and the last ones to pay anything." That struck Shmuel as immoral. If you want to receive, you have to give. "It's like a well; you have to put in water to get water." Shmuel may not have professed to be a Zionist, but he was not anti-Zionist, and he particularly didn't like seeing anti-Zionist religious organizations exploit the financial machinery of the Zionist state.

"In Europe the Communists were a fifth column. Here in Israel I can see about ten fifth columns. All Jews!" Included for Shmuel were the religious Jews in Meah Shearim (the ultra-orthodox neighborhood of Jerusalem). In general, Shmuel liked people but he thought that those who objected to the secular state (like some residents of the ultra-orthodox neighborhoods) shouldn't ask for welfare from the State. Then he recalled the speech given in Yiddish by the head of an important yeshiva at the Agudat Yisrael convention (the anti-Zionist religious political organization) that Shmuel heard on Israeli radio. Shmuel explained his opinion of those who don't accept the secular institutions of Israeli society.

"You can't talk to *Am Yisrael* (the Jewish people) like that, to come and say that *Zahal* (the Israeli armed forces) is not *Zahal*, the *chayalim* (soldiers) are not *chayalim*, and the land is not the land that God gave to the Jewish people. We're all one people, a folk in the *midbar* (desert)! You know what that means? That means if I am isolated in the *midbar*, I'm a businessman, I can send *zedakah* (charity) to my brothers and sisters." If you oppose the State of Israel, Shmuel thought, you should keep your hands out of the public coffers. "If the Jewish people are still wandering in the desert, not yet having entered the 'promised land,' then don't raise money abroad on the grounds that it's a big *mitzvah* (religious duty) to live and study in the holy land."

Shmuel wanted honesty and national unity, and it upset him when he found neither. "I'm very disappointed and confused. I don't understand how can in the State of Israel exist how many? Twenty and something political parties." We reminded him that in the Tarnow memorial volume it says that eight or nine political party lists contended in the elections for the leadership of the Jewish community. He didn't want to remember that the ideological divisions that mark

Israel politics were, in large part, inherited from Jewish communal politics in Europe. In Poland he felt the common concern that underlay the political contention, whereas in Israel he simply could not discern that solidarity.

Perhaps Shmuel would have felt closer to Israeli society if he spoke Hebrew. However, a person who knows English and Yiddish can keep well informed in Israel and find plenty of people to talk to. Shmuel regularly read the Yiddish paper and he listened to the Yiddish program every evening at 6:30 on Israeli radio. "That is a good program," he said, lively and comprehensive, and it kept its listeners in the know. Shmuel was a critical witness to current events. He thought that Israeli politics were merely personal squabbles with no ideological basis, and he supported his conclusion with many examples taken from the daily political reports on the radio.

On one occasion we met Shmuel at a meeting of the Association of Americans and Canadians in Israel. "What's a Polish Jew from Australia doing here?" we asked. He laughed. From the accent of a lot of the elderly Americans and Canadians at that meeting, it could just as well have been a meeting of the Bialystok Society in Melbourne. Shmuel felt right at home. He had come with some friends to hear a prominent member of the Knesset give a speech and answer questions about the involvement of citizens in projects for the improvement of the quality of life in Israel. The Knesset member, who spoke excellent English with an accent that indicated that he too could be addressing a meeting of the Bialystok Society in Yiddish, Polish, or Russian, drew Shmuel's fire, after the fact. "If my English was better, I would say something at that meeting. But I bite my tongue." Shmuel wanted to know, what kind of sense did it make to tell an audience composed mostly of retired people to become active in Israeli politics. Shmuel came to hear something else, apparently. But he couldn't tell us what it was.

Much of Shmuel's disappointment with Israeli life was an elderly man's cynicism, the moodiness of a man feeling his faculties slipping away. When he was tired he was very critical. When he was feeling lively, he was less so. However, he maintained consistently that the Jewish element of life in Israel lacked the spirit and intensity he remembered from his childhood in Tarnow. It's playacting with no sincerity, Shmuel declared. "You know the play, *The Dybbuk*, by Ansky?" he asked "I have seen this play three times. I saw it in Yiddish by the Vilna troupe. The Habimah came, and I saw it in Ivrit (Hebrew), with that actress that just died" (Hannah Rovina). And I saw it in Krakow at the

State Theater in Polish. With some Jews from Tarnow I go to Krakow. I have to see The *Dybbuk* in Polish. But I went home half way through. How can you say in Polish, '*Dybbuk, geh arois*' (Demon, get out!)? From Vilna to Habima is day and night. And from Vilna and Habima to Polish is a hundred and a hundred thousand miles away. That is to me *Yiddishkeit* now. The *Dybbuk* in Polish."

We asked him what he thought about Meah Shearim, which seems to us like a slice of Eastern European Jewish life transported to the Middle East with as much connection to the modern State of Israel as a Bedouin encampment. "No" Shmuel said. "What you can see in Meah Shearim is not comparable. They are like actors. You don't know that kind of people. I know that kind of people because I have seen it a lot. I haven't got that feeling in Meah Shearim." Shmuel thought that the Hasidic outfit, long black coats and round, fur hats, *shtraimels*, was merely a costume. "I once asked a Hasid what that clothes has to do with religion. A *shmata* is a *shmata* (a rag is a rag). He couldn't answer me. You know a *shtraimel* costs more than a thousand dollars?!" The ultra-orthodoxy in Israel seems to Shmuel to be superficial and artificial and he insisted that we not confuse the appearance of these Hasidim with the genuine article that he remembers from Tarnow.

Shmuel venerated the rabbis in Tarnow, and he had hoped to find people like that in Israel, but he thought people were heartless here. "Just *shpilen* (play-acting)." After his first marriage, Shmuel used to attend services at a tiny Hasidic synagogue because of a particular cantor. "When he was *davening* (leading the prayer service), I couldn't go out for one second. You haven't got the strength to go out. You was sitting just like nailed to the seat. He was crying all the time, not tears, but from the heart. He filled them up with something. You can't describe that. The cantor was seventy-five years old. Not one gray hair." In comparison, he found that the religious services in the synagogue he attended in Jerusalem were sterile.

Shmuel often complained about the way things were done in this synagogue. They put in new lighting fixtures, which reminded Shmuel of "a Spanish bordello." Shmuel couldn't stand the petty vying for honors and small-minded one-upmanship. His fellow worshipers were on display, one man insisting on starting two minutes early, and another one constantly arriving two minutes late and complaining. Also, the behavior of the *gabbayim*, the volunteers who administer the synagogue, offended him. They were self-important, which, we reminded Shmuel, was a *gabbay's* privilege. Nevertheless, it bothered Shmuel that they always discussed synagogue business during morning prayers and on Shabbat. "Can't they make time for a private meeting?"

He suspected that one of the *gabbayim* was a hypocrite. An unusual man, he was a member of a secular kibbutz that sits on the old Jordanian border, now within the city limits of Jerusalem, not far from the synagogue. Apparently, he had been raised in a religious home in some place like Tarnow. He rebelled and ran away to Palestine, joined a kibbutz, but as an elderly man, he became an observant Jew again. Once when Shmuel went to the kibbutz to buy some fruit, he looked up the *gabbay* and found him eating in the kibbutz dining hall. "Are you telling me that food is kosher?" Shmuel asked rhetorically. He didn't like the idea of a man putting on a big show at the synagogue and eating non-kosher food back home.

As for the rabbi of his synagogue in Jerusalem, Shmuel thought he was out of sync with the congregation. He was a young man, a political appointee like all neighborhood rabbis in Israel, without much in common with the community he was supposed to serve and little notion of how to address that community. Nevertheless, Shmuel's life in his neighborhood revolved around the synagogue. Most of his friends attended services with him. Without the synagogue, its vulgar chandeliers, its self-important, possibly hypocritical functionaries, and its young rabbi, Shmuel would have had few concerns to share with the people around him, little to gossip about, and even more reason to be disappointed in Israel.

Despite his regular involvement in the synagogue, he did not claim to be a religious man. When he called to mind the way truly religious Jews longed for the Holy Land for centuries, he professed to be shocked about what went on in that land now. At one glum moment he even claimed that had he known how disappointing Israel would be, he would have stayed in Australia.

His harsh pronouncements were belied by the way he led his life. Shmuel was a very active man. He cared intensely about the welfare of the other elderly people who lived in his apartment building. He did favors for his weaker neighbors, buying a newspaper for them, helping them around the house, and visiting them in the hospital when they fell ill. When his first grandson was an infant, every day, rain or shine, he would take the child for a three hour walk in his carriage. People noticed his devotion. He became a local neighborhood fixture, the man who always walked with his grandchild. In that way, Shmuel grew familiar with the neighborhood and a large part of the surrounding areas.

He enjoyed exploring, and he knew his way about Jerusalem quite well. Every week he and Esther went to the open air market closer to downtown Jerusalem, to stock up on produce. They found the stall where everything was sold for the cheapest prices going, and they became steady customers. Having sold outdoors in a market himself, Shmuel appreciated the professionalism of the owner of the stall, Rachamim, an Oriental Jew, and apparently Rachamim recognized Shmuel and treated him courteously.

Shmuel was small in stature but he remained very strong and unafraid of physical exertion. In the fall before we began meeting with him, he had taken it upon himself to paint his daughter's apartment in Arad. Later in the year he excused himself from an appointment he had made with us because he had agreed to help his friend paint an apartment in Jerusalem, and he had tired himself out more than he had expected. We teased him and asked wondered whether he would like to paint our apartment too. "Why not?" Shmuel joked back. Had we asked, he would have been delighted to help.

Shmuel's unhappiness with Israel was undoubtedly genuine, but when pressed, he admitted to being comfortable in Israel "in a way." He had some practical problems. The value of his pension from Australia had dwindled, because the cost of living rose more rapidly than the rate of exchange.

"But do you feel lonely in Israel?" we asked.

"No"

"Did you feel lonely in Melbourne?"

"Sometimes"

While he wouldn't call himself a Zionist, he did concede that the future of most Jewish communities in the world was bound up with the future of Israel. He remembered his feelings after the war.

"We looked around. We could see that the Jews were a different kind of people. Not in looks. How they are dressed. In behavior. Just going around like a 'hind in a dorf' (a stray dog). Afraid of something. Always afraid of something. You see two Italians, you know it's their land. We are strangers."

We never asked Shmuel directly whether he had ever lost that feeling in Australia or whether he ever had it there. There was no need to ask. During twenty-five years in Australia, Shmuel never once troubled to explore beyond the Melbourne area. The man who had been an enthusiastic tourist as a youth in provincial Poland restricted himself to a single metropolitan area in Australia. But his wanderlust was not dead, merely dormant. As soon as they reached

Israel, Shmuel and Esther began to travel restlessly throughout Israel. They would sometimes pass a taxi stand on Ben Yehuda Street in downtown Jerusalem and hear the drivers calling "Tel Aviv!! Tel Aviv!!" and impulsively take a ride. Shmuel visited all his relatives, saw all the sights and bathed in every body of water. As he grew older, he found that travel made him very tired, and it was very expensive, so he cut down, but against his will.

On one occasion, Shmuel took a bus ride in Jerusalem to visit a cousin in another part of town. The bus was very crowded and he was pushed and shoved while waiting for his stop. Once off the bus he realized he had been pickpocketed by some young boys on the bus and his wallet and money had been stolen. He was distraught. How could this happen among Jews in Jerusalem, he pondered. Naturally he was upset and for a long time he was angry at himself and at his situation in Jerusalem. So he lodged no formal complaint and simply went about his daily business. For Shmuel the robbery was more than losing money and losing face; it was a comment on the new generation and his own marginality. He repeated the story often especially when he felt unhappy in Israel.

Nevertheless, Shmuel and Esther came increasingly to feel a part of Jerusalem. They had friends, neighbors, and some family and were part of a network of Yiddish speaking immigrants. Whenever they returned from Arad, visiting their daughter, or from Tel Aviv, they nudged each other in excitement: "We're back in Yerushalayim!" Jerusalem was becoming home.

For Shmuel, celebrating the weekly Sabbath in Jerusalem was truly Shabbat. As much as he liked being with his grandchildren in Arad, he didn't like Shabbat there. Saturdays in Jerusalem are very tranquil. There is little traffic. You see people walking in every direction, on their way to synagogue, on their way home, or on their way to visit friends. Shmuel valued the special feeling of Shabbat in Jerusalem. It was one of the few things he found that genuinely reminded him of Tarnow.

One of Shmuel's friends, an older man who had been very sick, kept asking him about Olam HaBah, the world to come. What is it like? What's there as an attraction? Shmuel put the man off. "Give me a ticket back, and I'll go and see for you."

Tradition has it that if you die in the Land of Israel, you are assured of a place in the world to come. Shmuel denied that he moved there for that reason.

Nor did he go to the synagogue to secure a place in heaven. "I go because I like to hear good *davening*, a good *baal koreh* (reader of the Torah)."

He turned to us, "You notice the difference when I sit next to you and when I *daven* (pray) for the whole *shul*? When I *daven* (as a prayer leader), I am careful, because I am *davening* for everybody." We suggested that he should *daven* (lead prayers) more often, since he was distracted when he sat next to us and talked to us rather than *daven*. Shmuel just smiled, knowing that he enjoyed both leading the religious services and sharing his stories with us.

Chapter Eight

"Not Lonely but Lost"

On the train home from Siberia to Tarnow, Galicia, Shmuel Braw planned to rebuild his life. He had been born, brought up, and married in Tarnow. He had owned a flourishing lumber and coal business there. In 1918, after four years in Hungary and Moravia as a refugee, their father had reestablished the business in Tarnow. In 1946, Shmuel was repatriated from Uzbekistan by the Soviet authorities, and he imagined he could do what his father had done. People would need coal and lumber in post-war Poland. Shmuel knew the business well. He would win back old customers.

He had lived through other momentous historical changes. He was born a subject of the Austro-Hungarian Empire. He had come of age and married in independent Poland. Now the Nazis had been defeated. The Polish government in exile was one of the Allies. Shmuel had survived for two and a half years in the Tarnow ghetto, and two and a half years more in a Siberian labor camp. He had nearly died of typhus. Now, at thirty-nine, fully recovered from the disease and nearly back up to his normal weight, he was on his way home. He would take up the life that the war had disrupted and live it out in his home town.

True, his only child, a ten-year old girl had died with other ghetto schoolchildren. True he had seen hundreds of Jews murdered, and had served on labor brigades, piling corpses into mass graves. True, his wife had been transported out of Tarnow in 1940 on her way to Auschwitz. But then Auschwitz was known as a large Nazi labor camp, not a synonym for genocide. Since Shmuel had survived in Siberia, where the conditions were incomparably worse than in the ghetto when he had escaped, it seemed reasonable for him to expect that his wife would be on another train heading towards Tarnow from Auschwitz.

The trip westward took three weeks. The train brought about six-hundred Polish Jews back from Central Asia. They were not prepared for what they found:

"Nothing, a cemetery."

Shmuel's voice sounds as if his mouth was still full of gall.

"The whole city was a cemetery. I mean the Jewish part. Nothing. Doesn't exist."

Now he is angry

"From the buildings is left only roofs, no windows, no doors, rubbish, rubble. Everywhere the streets are full of that. Nothing. Nothing."

When one thinks of the Holocaust, one thinks mainly of the murders, an inconceivable number of individual murders. One forgets the destruction of property, of monuments and community buildings, of houses, synagogues, schools, clubs, hospitals, shops: the material creation of tight-knit communities that had dwelt in one spot for centuries. Shmuel was a man with a highly developed sense of place, and his place had been utterly destroyed! Even before reliable information about the extent of the tragedy was available, the physical annihilation of the Jewish half of the town told Shmuel everything about what he needed to do in the future.

He stayed in Tarnow for five or six months, housed by the Jewish Welfare Organization in some buildings on the outskirts of the ghetto—Jewish property recovered after the war.

"Maybe the owners were dead," Shmuel speculates.

"How did you feel?"

"You are not lonely," he tells us. His voice is strangled, the words are almost swallowed.

"You are not lonely, but lost. You follow me, or not?"

Then he gives us his description of apathy:

"People without...without life. You want nothing. You want just death."

His voice strains, "Without feeling to anything. And that was with everybody the same."

Then one feeling emerged: the overpowering need to leave Poland as soon as possible.

Others had plans for Shmuel. He spoke good German; perfect Polish, and some Russian in addition to his native Yiddish. The Polish authorities offered him an important job in the administration of Silesia, the province that had been chopped off of Germany and presented to Poland in compensation for the eastern territories ceded to the USSR. The government had to fill up new land with Poles. Shmuel knew better than to turn down the offer immediately, although he admitted no intention of accepting it.

Agents of the Haganah in Poland also had plans for Shmuel. They wanted to get him to Palestine. He wasn't sure. He had never considered living in Palestine. He did have a sister and a brother there, but he would wait to hear from them before embarking. He committed himself only to use the Jewish underground organization to get out of Poland.

"Were you shocked when you first got back to Tarnow?" We asked naively to provoke some reaction from Shmuel and to better understand his feelings. "Shocked?" he asks, indulgently, with a smile he reserves for a particularly silly question. "What do you mean, 'shocked'? I couldn't sleep a week's time! I was wandering around. I couldn't go to bed. You know, I was in that street where I lived with my first wife and child about a dozen times."

His voice lowered to almost a whisper.

"And up to the house where I was living. And I couldn't go in."

It had been a rented apartment in a neighborhood that was not walled in when the Nazis created the ghetto. Many of Shmuel's belongings were probably still there. But he couldn't force himself over the threshold.

One afternoon Shmuel was wandering the streets of Tarnow near the former Jewish neighborhood. He ended up across from his former house only to see a woman whom he knew leave his previous home, with a black striped shawl covering her shoulders and arms. Shmuel just stared at her and the shawl. His eyes were burning; his throat was parched; Shmuel was in a state of shock and disbelief. Was this his prayer shawl, his tallis, with some of the fringes removed? Was this what had become of the one of the powerful symbols of his Jewish life? His Jewish life in Tarnow? He was certain it had been his but no longer was. He said to us tearfully with a choked voice, "just like Tarnow. The tallis was no longer mine."

His mother's house also stood on the edge of the ruins that had been the ghetto. He walked by it more than a dozen times, but again, he couldn't go in. He did enter his eldest sister's house because he had a good reason. She and her husband had been prosperous before the war. Shmuel always speaks of his eldest sister with great respect. He admired her almost as much as his father. Her house, a new one, was now occupied by a Polish family. Shmuel went in to talk to the new "lady of the house," and he was appalled to see his sister's furniture, intact and arranged in the same way. He says that, trudging back to his room, some five kilometers, "excuse me, I was vomiting all the way back. I was *mishigga*; I was sure I was finished. I was sick a week's time in bed."

While talking about his sister's house, he slapped the arms of his chair and twisted about. His mouth tightened. His voice got louder. How did the Polish woman come to occupy his sister's home? we asked.

"She bought it."

His brother-in-law's relatives, or purported relatives, appeared and sold the house quite legally. Shmuel is still angry at the pair of opportunists, brothers from the Tarnow area who showed up and posed as the surviving relatives of many missing Jews, pocketing the proceeds of legal sales without any regard for the actual living relatives: in Shmuel's case, his sister's two daughters in Palestine. He located the older of the pair and demanded that he return the Polish woman's money and annul the sale:

"No contract anymore. I'm here. I'm her brother.

"'How are you related?' I said, 'You know, *vi a knappa tsu de hoisen*' (like a button on a pair of pants)."

It turned out that the brothers were not the only opportunists in on the deal. One of the others had long since skipped town, and another was a cousin of Shmuel's brother-in-law. He was living in an all-Polish village some twenty-five kilometers away. During the war a Polish Catholic woman had hidden him. In gratitude, apparently, he had converted to Catholicism and married the woman. It was dangerous to go there, so Shmuel took along a young Jewish soldier. "I wanted somebody behind me with a revolver."

When they reached the town a crowd gathered, and soon everyone knew a Jew had arrived. Shmuel asked directions to the convert's home, refusing to say why he had come to see him. He knocked on the door. A woman's voice invited them to come in. The walls were covered with crosses and holy pictures. Again, Shmuel refused to say what he wanted, insisting only that it had nothing to do with her husband's conversion. The woman said her husband was out. She would go find him.

"I said to the soldier, 'Either she went to get some people to beat us up, so be prepared, or she went to get him.'"

Shmuel paused dramatically to build up the suspense for us. If he could have spoken to us freely in Yiddish and not struggled to find the right English words, what a flow of language we would have heard!

Shmuel had never been afraid of Poles. Before the war he had employed some fifty Polish workmen, and he had operated freely all over the countryside near Tarnow, cutting timber and hauling it. But in 1946, there were areas where a Jew couldn't go. For six years the Jews had not only been deprived of the protection they had formerly enjoyed as Polish citizens with civil rights, but the German occupiers had encouraged Poles to murder Jews. After the war several more pogroms took place in Poland. For a Jew, it was no longer the same country.

Shmuel and the young soldier sat and waited in the rustic room full of crosses. Time passed slowly. The woman finally came back with her husband. He recognized Shmuel right away. Pleased to see him, the apostate started speaking in Yiddish. Shmuel stopped him.

"Speak in Polish so that your wife will understand everything that we say."

Shmuel reassured him that he didn't care what religion he was. Even today there is no hint of condemnation or reproach in his account of the man. While explaining what he had come for, he kept his eye on the woman:

"I was observing her face, her reaction. She turned red like ink, like blood. Her eyes were full of blood. Uh oh! Here! I just pushed the button!"

The husband calmed his wife down and agreed to meet Shmuel in Tarnow the next day to settle the matter.

Shmuel got a small amount of money from him and was advised not to try to renegotiate the contract. He returned to the older of the brothers who had been in on the deal and threatened him. Shmuel was well-known in Tarnow, also among the gentiles. He said he was not afraid to go to the police, or reluctant to turn to the Jewish Welfare Organization.

"I will come back with some people and demolish everything in your flat if you don't give me the money."

His voice was furious as he told the story. The man gave him some money and told him that his brother had the rest. Shmuel located him and threatened to kill him if he didn't pay up.

"I have got no more scruples," he explained to us.

He saw it as his moral duty to recover his nieces' money, and he was undeterred even by the younger brother's announcement that he had a revolver in his pocket.

"I was naive," he told us.

The younger brother promised to pay him, but he just skipped town. Shmuel's anger remained as strong as ever.

At least he had raised some money for his nieces. He eventually brought the money across three borders to Rome. From there he sent sewing machines, radios, and things like that to Palestine. In 1975 he saw what he had sent, when he moved to Israel from Australia.

Shmuel settled another account while he was back in Poland. Amon Göth, the Gestapo commandant who had organized the destruction of the Jewish community of Tarnow was tried in Krakow. Shmuel made a special trip to see the man hanged. He was still proud to have witnessed the small act of just retribution, although it was no compensation for the destruction for the Jewish half of the city and the murder of most of its Jewish population..

The Christian parts of Tarnow were virtually intact after the war. Shmuel had a large number of Christian business associates and childhood friends. One whom he mentioned was a man named Roman. They had gone to the same school, and their fathers had done a lot of business together. Roman's father owned a flour mill, and Shmuel's father, who maintained a warehouse adjoining the mill, used to sell him coal and wood and lend him money from time to time. Roman insisted that Shmuel come out to visit him, and Shmuel told him he would come the next day. He had to find out whether his Polish friend was still trustworthy.

Shmuel's Jewish sources told him he could rely on Roman. In fact, Roman's family had hidden eight Jews for the duration of the war in the great chimney of an abandoned mill. Two of Roman's four brothers were killed by the Germans, perhaps as partisans.

Shmuel didn't tell us what he was thinking on the way to Roman's, unaccountably a vulnerable alien in his native city. How could he help compare his situation with his friend's? Both had suffered losses, but the Polish Catholic could carry on. The Polish Jew could only leave.

Roman took a close look at Shmuel's clothes. Before the war Shmuel had been a natty dresser. Now he was wearing an odd assortment of cast-off garments. He had received them by mistake in a parcel sent from America to

Uzbekistan. "Do you need any clothes?" he asked. Shmuel declined. Roman opened a wardrobe and showed Shmuel some thirty suits. The two men were roughly the same size. "Take five or six suits," Roman said, "I made a lot of money during the war. I can have another suit made in five minutes." Shmuel declined. Roman insisted, "If you don't take them with you, I will bring them to your flat tomorrow." There was no evading Roman's generosity, so Shmuel took three suits, some shirts and some underwear—a whole suitcase full of clothes. He drew the line at shoes, though. He said he wouldn't have felt comfortable in another man's shoes.

Shmuel has some pictures taken in Tarnow in 1946. One shows a broken column with Hebrew letters carved on it. The survivors erected a memorial in the Jewish cemetery, where, as Shmuel has said several times, 24,000 Jews are buried in eight mass graves. He pauses and repeats the figure so it will sink in. Eight pits with 3,000 corpses in each one of them.

The picture of the memorial didn't affect us much: a broken pillar from the New Synagogue with a simple inscription. We had seen too many memorials. We were more shaken when we heard that every Jewish survivor in Tarnow placed a stone in the commemorative wall visible behind the pillar. "On my stone there were seventeen names," Shmuel told us. That is a statistic one can grasp.

Seven close relatives: his wife and daughter, two sisters, their husbands, several of their children, one brother, his sister-in-law, their twin sons, another sister-in-law and her children, some of his many cousins. An extended family was reduced to a handful of isolated survivors.

What was left of Shmuel's Tarnow? The Jewish houses and institutions no longer stand. Nine-tenths of the Jews who lived there were murdered. Those who survived now live in dozens of foreign cities on every continent. The close-knit society that shaped Shmuel's personality and fostered his development was ripped to shreds. Shmuel was one of its tattered remnants, and he still yearned for the whole cloth from which he was torn.

Shmuel never lost his vitality, however. He showed us another photograph. It is of himself, neat, clean, well-dressed, probably in one of Roman's suits. Next to him, smiling shyly, is an attractive young woman, Esther, his second wife. They don't look as if they'd just survived a holocaust. We looked at the face in the picture and at the seventy-three year old man before us, and we remembered all he had told us about the ghetto, about Siberia and about Tarnow.

It was the same face, features altered by time, of course, but we couldn't make the connection easily between the man we knew, the stories we heard, and the determined face in the thirty-four year old picture.

We asked Shmuel whether he thought it was normal to want to remarry under those circumstances, nearly crushed by the weight of catastrophe, with no clear plans for the future. He equivocated: "Normal, and not normal."

Esther had appeared in Uzbekistan toward the end of the war with a small group of young Ukrainian Jews, following rumors of their relatives' survival. Her village had been completely destroyed. When the repatriation began, she and some other people with no where else to go joined up with Shmuel.

In Tarnow, Esther met a man from her town, and he warned her against trying to make her way back there. Not only was there nothing left to recover, but, "You can be killed any minute," the man said. Esther announced to Shmuel, "Don't tell me anything, I'm staying in Tarnow." But she was deeply depressed. She sat for hours and stared at the walls. Shmuel took care of her. He brought her clothes to replace the rags they'd brought back from Russia. He helped her because she was lost, not because he expected to marry her.

She responded to his attention, though. "I just brought her back to life." He sighed, "To say the truth, I was quite a bit older, sixteen years older than she was, a married man. I lost my wife and child. Still, she was a young girl I told you. She was a beautiful girl, very attractive. I never speak to her about marriage, because what kind of chance do I have? She will meet somebody, a younger man, and she will marry him."

It had taken Shmuel less than ten days to propose to his first wife. He had been a decisive young man with his prospects well in hand. Fifteen years later he thought he had nothing to offer a young woman.

One day he found Esther sitting in the apartment where the Jewish Welfare Organization had housed them, "a few boys in this room, a few girls in that, just like a community." He told her about the job offered to him by the Polish government, and that he no intention of going to Silesia. He said he planned to leave Poland. "What will you do?" he asked her. She didn't know. Then she said, "Take me with you."

As he retold it, Shmuel was a bit embarrassed. He felt that it was wrong for an unmarried couple to travel together, and he didn't want to give the impression that either he or Esther had that in mind. "'What do you mean?' I asked her 'I can't take you with me because we are not married, and I'm older than you, nearly twice as old.' She answered, 'What's the trouble?' Just like that, 'We'll get married. I haven't got anybody. I know you. I trust you. I like you.'"

The rabbis of Tarnow had all been murdered very early in the Nazi occupation. Among the repatriated Jews there was a young rabbi. "He said he was a rabbi," Shmuel commented, with a tinge of skepticism. He and Esther asked the young man to marry them. Now, in order for a Jewish marriage to take place, Shmuel had to prove that his first wife had died. Fortunately, one of Tarnow's Jews, a man named Asher, had escaped from Auschwitz. His job there had been unloading the deportees' personal belongings from the railway cars, and he was able to sneak onto a train as it pulled out of the concentration camp. He and another man escaped together. They leaped from the train as it was passing through a forest, and eventually joined a band of partisans. Asher was able to testify that the first Mrs. Braw was dead. His was the painful task of giving a great deal of such testimony.

Esther's case was more complex. The rabbi needed witnesses that Esther was both Jewish and unmarried. Not one of Esther's relatives had survived, no one from her town in the Ukraine was available to testify in Tarnow, and, even had communication been possible, no Jews were left there to question. Shmuel persuaded the rabbi to perform the ceremony. When recollecting the arguments he used, he switched to Yiddish. He mingled threats with logic. He believed Esther. After all, he was the one who was going to marry her. Besides, would the rabbi have him leave her alone? "I can't just leave her on the street!" Finally, if the rabbi refused to perform the ceremony, they would make do with a civil marriage, Shmuel argued. No matter what, Shmuel and Esther intended to leave Poland together as man and wife.

That was their only hope for living a normal life. "I will do everything I can to get out," says Shmuel, remembering his thinking in 1946. "You can't live in a cemetery." He and other survivors in Tarnow "saw that they had to come back to a normal life. You know what I mean? You fell in the mud. But you can't stay dirty all your life. True or not?" Then he quotes from a popular Yiddish poem "*Di Goldene Kait*," (the Golden Chain). You have to keep adding links to the golden chain. That was a theme of their discussions at night. They weren't prepared to give up.

What made Shmuel want to live after what he had seen? He pondered a response since he took our provocatively blunt question seriously. It was legitimate to wonder about such things, he told us. "First thing, you've got a feeling, that they won't destroy the Jewish people. We wanted to build back up a Jewish life to what it was in Poland."

He and Esther made their way, mainly on foot with thousands of others, across the Czech border, then into Austria, and finally to Italy, where they awaited individual solutions to their problems, destinations to put an end to their displacement.

Although he maintains a cheerful, charming manner, Shmuel is troubled. "What you see, what you go through. You are not a piece of wood, or a stone. You've got some brains." He puts both hands on his head. "I mean not very bright ones, but you're thinking about things, and you see a different life. It's coming to you that something has changed. Something that doesn't exist. Now I have just *tsvaifeln* (doubts) about a lot of things. I wouldn't think about that for one second in Tarnow." With Esther in hand, Shmuel embarked on another leg of his life's journey, into the unknown.

Chapter Nine

"A Normal Life"

Shmuel spent three years in Italy, but at first he only mentioned three months of them, during which he slept in a bathtub in Milan. "I had to go to the office of ORT, (acronym of the Russian words meaning The Society for Trades and Agricultural Labor, a veteran Jewish self-help organization) and there I meet a man, Dr. Yaffa, and you know I got to know a lot of different kinds of people after the war. He was a man maybe in his eighties, but he looked like a man of sixty. One time I make a mistake and I ask him, 'How old you are?' And he said, 'I don't know. Ask the documents, they know.' I see that I have made a mistake in asking him that."

"Dr. Yaffa asked me if I am from Poland and we have a chat. He never mentioned anything special, but my name rings a bell with him. He invites me home to supper, and I don't know why I suspect something. Not something bad; it had to do with war."

The Yaffas had lived in Poland during the war, disguised as gentiles. They were tall and blond, like Christians, and they spoke perfect Polish. Dr. Yaffa's sister asked Shmuel where he was born and whether he had a brother in Lvov. It turned out that Shmuel's brother Yitshak-Ignatz had stayed with the Yaffa family in Lvov until the Gestapo arrested him. "That's how I find out what happened to him."

Dr. Yaffa was the director of the ORT vocational schools. He needed a trustworthy purchasing agent. Shmuel tried to turn the job down. It would be too hard. His wife and daughter were in Rome. Dr. Yaffa insisted and prevailed, so Shmuel began working in Milan. However, he couldn't find a place to stay. As a special favor, the manager of a hotel let him sleep in a bathtub, but since he couldn't possibly bring his family to live in a lavatory, he reluctantly quit. He didn't need the salary so much because he was receiving support from the UNWRO and the Joint Distribution Committee, but it had felt good to hold a job. "I wanted to work."

Shmuel passed his job over to a cousin and went back to Rome with some packages of food and twelve cartons of American cigarettes ("They were worth a fortune!") in lieu of severance pay.

Esther and Shmuel had made their way from Poland to Italy in trucks but mainly by foot. The Jewish underground organization in Poland brought them to the Czechoslovak border in trucks. The climbed out of the trucks and the border guards waved them across in friendly fashion, confirming Shmuel's good opinion of the Czechs. "They knew we were not going to stay there." The refugees were transported across Czechoslovakia to the Austrian border, where the guards were bribed to look the other way. There were thousands of Jewish refugees on the road, streaming southward with the aid and encouragement of the Jewish Agency and the Zionist organization Bricha. The aim was to bring them to Palestine, either by pressing the British to admit them legally, or by embarrassing the British by forcing them to turn away the homeless survivors of Hitler's genocide at the very gates of the Promised Land.

The Braws spent several months in a transit camp in Austria, in the spring of 1946. That is where they celebrated their first post-war Passover Seder. Shmuel does not remember it as a joyous occasion. Rather than a feeling of solidarity in distress, the refugees felt cut off from each other, suspicious, worried about the future and overwhelmed with miserable loneliness.

They were moved on to Italy. At the border, the guards had been bribed again, this time to stand in a shallow vale and look eastward while hundreds of Jews climbed over a low hill toward the west. Trucks drove to the border and picked up the illegal immigrants.

We were puzzled: after what Shmuel had been through, wasn't he afraid or at least hesitant to get on trucks and be taken somewhere by people he didn't know? Shmuel thought for a while and dismissed the notion. "In the first place, we got no option. Are we going to stay at the border? And also we trust them. The drivers are Italians, but the people in charge are Jews like we were. And there are hundreds of people behind you. You have to get up on the truck."

They were driven to a disused army base in a town called Grugliasco, near Turin. "There we met our first Israeli" (he meant a Jew from Palestine), Shmuel told us with a sour expression on his face. "His name was Aryeh. To us he looks like a Gestapo man. He has new boots, and they are always polished. He is wearing a uniform, and he is carrying a little stick. It makes me feel shaky." The conditions in the new camp were unacceptable. The first night there were not enough blankets. People slept in their clothes, and still they were freezing cold. The next morning they received a miserable breakfast: cold coffee, a stale roll, and rancid peanut butter. "Esther was already pregnant. How could they give people such bad food? We were cold. Not even hot coffee?"

The refugees sent a delegation to Aryeh. Shmuel was among them. "I just listen. I never spoke. I was shocked to hear that we are not allowed to leave. There were guards. Yiddishe guards."

Shmuel sized up Aryeh right away and decided that he would leave camp with Esther the next day. Meanwhile, he had to get some food. He walked over to the gate of the camp, where an indistinct group of men had gathered. He stood around for ten minutes or so as if he were one of those watching the inmates to prevent them from sneaking out. Then he simply walked out the gate and nobody tried to stop him.

"I just start walking the streets, looking for shops. I have dollars still from Tarnow, you remember." He had learned the Italian word for bread before setting out. He saw a line in front of a bakery and joined it. He was the only one without a ration card. When his turn came, "I *pane-ed* maybe five minutes. The salesgirl asked me for the tickets. I just shrug and say '*pane*.' The girl went to an older woman. She asked, '*straniero*?' I talk to her in German. I know that a lot of Italians speak German. After the war you can kill them, they won't speak German. So finally they give me half a loaf of bread and half a dozen rolls. They won't take money from me. They say, '*va bene, va bene*' I don't know what to do. I don't want to go and not pay, but they won't take my dollar. They push me out of the shop."

Down the street Shmuel found a cheese shop where they took his American money and gave him Italian money in change. He brought the bread and cheese back to the camp and ate it with Esther and a few of their friends. Aryeh came in as they were eating and asked them angrily, 'Who brought the food? How did you get out of the camp? It's forbidden to leave. You do it once more, and you'll be in trouble with me once more!' Shmuel switched into Yiddish as he recalled his argument with Aryeh.

"Aryeh didn't want to get in trouble with the Italian government. That was the arrangements the Jewish organizations had made in Italy. Getting into the camp was easy. Getting out was the difficult part."

Shmuel's escapade benefited the whole group, because the next day the food improved, but he still had no intention of staying there. He had privately shipped all of his belongings from Tarnow to Rome, not trusting the Jewish Agency to take care of them. In fact, Shmuel claimed, the people who sent packages through the refugee organizations never recovered them. He believed they were all sent on to Palestine and distributed to needy people there. "It makes a bad feeling, you know. If they ask us, we will say yes, of course. But it is not nice to do it without asking."

He told Esther they were leaving the camp, and she didn't believe him. Undeterred, Shmuel roved around the camp looking for a sympathetic looking official "an *eigener* (one of our own). He will understand me very good." Shmuel explained about his shipment to Rome, that he had contacts there, and the man helped him and Esther leave the camp without Aryeh's knowledge.

At the railroad station they waited for the southbound train, and when it came it was mobbed. People were crushed in the corridors, jammed into the compartments, and hanging out of the doors and windows. But Shmuel noticed some empty cars, second class carriages. He brought Esther into one of them. "What can happen?"

They were too prudent to take seats in a compartment. They settled on folding chairs near a window in the corridor. Shmuel hadn't bought tickets, but he did have a lot of Italian money. The conductor came and said, '*Bigletto*?'

"I just shrug and he went away. But I got some money ready. The conductor came back with an inspector, and he brought with him a gentleman who speaks German, a very nice man." Shmuel's voice took on added warmth as he remembered the Italian "gentleman." The inspector only took the price of a third class ticket after he learned who Esther and Shmuel were, but he warned them that at two o'clock a stricter inspector would come on.

Before going off duty, the inspector came back and led Esther and Shmuel to seats in the third class section, explaining to the other passengers that they were Jewish refugees from Poland and that Esther was pregnant. "The people give us food. Everybody offered food. That's what the Italians are like."

The railroad station in Rome made a fabulous impression on Shmuel. He had not been in such a splendid edifice for ages. But it was bedlam, crowded with thousands of people rushing about and making a hubbub. He and Esther stood in complete bewilderment with no idea how to make their way out of the station. The Italian gentlemen who had assisted them in the train sought them out and came to their rescue again. Shmuel had an address, the pension where a friend of his was staying. The gentleman took Shmuel and Esther to the bus and spoke to the driver, then he said goodbye to the couple and wished them well. Whenever Shmuel moved to get off the bus, the driver signaled to him to stay on. After a long ride, he stopped the bus in the middle of a block and told Shmuel and Esther to get off. He left them right at the door of the pension.

As it happened, Shmuel's friend, who was an officer in the Polish army, had just been sent to England. The landlord put them up in a small room and took very little rent. "The Italians were very helpful to me," Shmuel explained, "because they suffered a lot from the Germans too." He and Esther stayed in the pension for nine days, but he felt wrong in exploiting the landlord's generosity for so long. He also didn't want to squander his nieces' money. He found an acquaintance from Tarnow in the market in Rome, and through him he learned of the big refugee camp run by the Joint in Cinecittà, the moving picture industry center southeast of Rome.

The conditions in Cinecittà were good. At the same time people were being temporarily settled in villas rented by the Joint, larger houses that had either been confiscated by the government or had become too expensive for individual families to maintain. Shmuel and Esther joined a group to whom a villa was assigned. "You got everything, central heating, a beautiful villa, but there are also problems. Ten, twelve families using the same kitchen, for example. We had room for sixty people, but we are very careful who we take. Some of the people were just vandals. They are destroying the houses. They couldn't get back to normal life. Camp people. We decided to make something special. We made like a kibbutz. We elected a committee. I was in charge of buying the food and things. I got contact with everybody. I go to the Joint twice a week. We had sixty beds, army beds, wool blankets, sheets, everything. They give us cigarettes. We decide to organize a kitchen for everyone. We are selling the extra cigarettes on the black market, and we are buying food. We started out with thirty people. Asher, from Tarnow, he was the cook."

The women took turns helping in the kitchen, and Shmuel's "kibbutz" became a model for the others in Rome. All of its members had a strong desire to return to normalcy. They started using their skills. One of the men was a tailor, and he taught the others. Soon they had a combination vocational school and cut-rate tailor shop going. They also had a photographer. There was a lot of work. They got welfare money from the government and pooled it for their collective needs, distributing what was left over. Shmuel also traded the canned goods they received from welfare organizations for fresh vegetables. "We start to eat normally. Not like in the camp."

The Braws' older daughter, Rivka, was born in Rome, the first child in the group, a cause for great rejoicing, At the end there were more than sixty people, including four children. "We squashed in another five people. You can't make a swindle. Everyone has to be registered. We had a normal life. We don't want to be *shnorrers* anymore. Whenever *machers* (big shots) come to Rome to see what the Joint is doing, they come to visit our kibbutz."

"Did it have a name?" we asked.

"Yes, *Aufbau* (Reconstruction). I have pictures from the kibbutz. I will bring them next time." But in fact, he never brought them.

Shmuel lost contact with people from his Rome Kibbutz. None of them went the route that Shmuel and his family took to Australia. Most went on to Palestine. Did Shmuel ever regret not going directly to Palestine?

"Gradually things changed, and people got the opportunity to go to a lot of places: Canada, South Africa. I wanted to go to Palestine. It's the normal thing to be with my family. My family was here. My brother, my sister. But my brother who came with the Andersarmee (Ander's Army) to Palestine—he just disappeared one day from the army; the military police looked for him, but he just disappeared in Israel—he wrote letters saying it was very hard in Israel. 'You went through hell. If you got a possibility to make your life easy, go for a few years. Then you'll come.'"

So Shmuel didn't expect to spend twenty-seven years in Melbourne. "Of course not. But I had to leave Italy. Either go to Palestine or back to Poland, or where you like. Italy couldn't afford it anymore." Shmuel was evidently hoping that the situation in Italy would change for the better, and that he could stay.

We wondered how Shmuel felt when he heard that the State of Israel had been established. "We heard it on the radio. We were in contact with all the organizations." In trying to identify his reaction, Shmuel's voice sounded dubious. He had to search for his words.

"Some was happy." But he didn't say "happy" in a happy way. "Some was half happy. Some was indifferent." Shmuel straightened in his seat and leaned forward, explaining himself.

"Listen, if the Jewish people lived for so many years without a country, we haven't got a feeling to have a country, you know what I mean? It was something strange. It was unbelievable. We couldn't understand how they would manage in that country. First thing, it was only a little over half a million people. They have to have a police. They have to have everything. And then there are the wars with the Arabs. Just how they can manage to manage a country? Because six hundred thousand people. That's a city, but not a country."

He sat back but kept groping for an appropriate expression. "It was a meal you never tasted. True, if you lived for generation after generation in Poland or Russia, you haven't got a feeling for your own country. What kind of a *geshmak dos hot*" (what it tastes like). Shmuel continued, "I can tell you the feeling from the people. They say it's something they don't believe in that it's here. They had no confidence. People didn't have the feeling that Israel would make it. A few maybe did. They say in Polish, when you come in a company of crooks, you have to play with them. You can't be a saint with crooks. Because they throw you out in a minute." In Polish he told us the proverb, which he haltingly translated: "You've got to caw with the crows."

"The feeling was very cold. And another thing. They have seen people coming from Israel, the *shlichim* (official emissaries), how they manage with people. You know, the way they treated them. Like Aryeh. They said, 'that people was hard people.' They got, after suffering, they need something that you heal them. But if you put on a wound salt, it hurts. And everybody was wounded. True? Everybody was hurt, and they put salt on them. So they reacted negatively. Of course! They were against that. They started to fight that. That's life. And another thing, it's coming, little things, the luggage."

Here Shmuel again complained that the Jewish Agency simply took the refugees' belongings and never returned them, sending them on to Palestine instead.

"In a way they were right, but the way they did it was wrong. It's not much, but it's important to people that got nothing at all. A shirt? It's a fortune. You haven't got it for years."

Shmuel's encounter with Italy was a mixed experience. With uncanny commitment to a normal life, he survived less than ideal conditions in Italy, and he made them better. His encounters with a soon-to-be Israeli bureaucracy and soon-to-become Israeli bureaucrats were less satisfying, and a quarter of a century would pass before he would reconnect with them in Israel.

Chapter Ten

New Places

Shmuel's life has taken him many places, most of them inaccessible. Jewish Tarnow no longer exists. Berlin of the Weimar Republic is a city of the remote past. The Tarnow Ghetto under the Nazis is a nightmare that does not fit into our picture of the common human world. We know it happened, but in its cruelty and insanity, we cannot encompass it. The Siberian labor camp, about which we can read elsewhere, characterizes an alien, tyrannical regime. Where is Siberia? Where is Uzbekistan? Where is Bukhara? Those are places beyond our reach. (In fact, Jeff traveled to Uzbekistan with his wife in the late 1990s, but that could give him only the slightest idea of what Bukhara might have been like under Soviet rule during World War II.) But when Shmuel got to Rome, he entered a world of which we have some inkling. We have been to Rome. We have seen movies set in post-war Italy. We know servicemen who were stationed there during and after the war. Yet, Shmuel's experience in Rome also remains beyond our grasp.

He and Esther had finally escaped from violence, terror, and immediate danger to their lives. They were living with their fellow Jews, protected, supported and no longer on the run Their lives had returned to the sphere in which we live, the sphere of civil order. Nevertheless, their future was still entirely uncertain. Their lives were directionless.

Shmuel seems to have had a capacity for leadership. He put together a group of friends and stole out of the ghetto with them. In his pre-trial detention, he exerted an influence on the men about him and helped them bear the discomfort and uncertainty. In the labor camp he was among those whom the men sent to deal with the authorities, a crew foreman, not a mere worker. In Central Asia a group formed about him and followed him back to Tarnow. In the refugee camp in Grugliasco, Shmuel was also among the men who negotiated with the authorities, and in his Roman villa he was one of the group's leaders.

He was a leader, but with a dwindling following and no charted course—a natural leader with no intention of leading. Like everyone else, he looked for an individual solution to his problems. The collectivity was a transient state. Shmuel had a wife and an infant. He was not a young man, he had no material resources, and his future was still very cloudy. Compare his position to what it had been in 1931 when he first married. Then he had been a vigorous man of twenty-five, well-known in his home town, and employed in a prospering family business. His future seemed to offer him steady progress towards wealth, comfort and influence: an enviable prospect. Sixteen years later, as he entered into a second marriage, what could he reasonably expect? There was no way of knowing. He did not know where he would settle, what new language he would have to learn, or how he could support himself. Shmuel was never afraid of hard work, and in his talks with us, he expressed pride in his ability to labor for long hours. In Poland at his age he would have had the prospect of easing off and passing some of the burden on to a nephew or son-in-law. After the war, it was clear there would be no let-up.

Shmuel did not do some of the things one might have expected him to do. With the nine hundred dollars he had brought from Poland and the goods he received as a refugee, Shmuel might have been able to make a lot of money in the black market. After all, his nieces neither knew about the money nor expected it. He could have paid them back with interest in a year or two. But Shmuel sent it off as soon as he could, in the form of sewing machines and other material goods. He seems to have formed no permanent ties with any of his fellow refugees; connections upon which he might have built a future for himself. He did not fall back on his family in Palestine or America. He also seems to have made no preparations for emigration to Australia. He did not study English, and he made no effort to find much about his new country. It sounds as if Shmuel became passive in Italy, that he had lost his energetic optimism after years of improvising daring solutions to impossible problems, of outsmarting officials, and of fighting for survival.

By 1949, Shmuel had been cut-off from his former, normal life for ten full years, ten irregular, unpredictable, trying years: three years under Nazi occupation, four years in the USSR, and then three years as a displaced person. Today, if an executive loses his job and has to spend half a year or more searching for a new one, he is the subject of concern. How can he bear the uncertainty, the blow to his identity connected with loss of position, the financial drain? How, then, did Shmuel bear the loss, the destruction of his former self, and the uncertainty of his future? One gathers that in Italy Shmuel waited for someone else to come along and solve some of his basic problems. While he was waiting he and Esther enjoyed Italy.

Once when they dropped in together in our home in Talpiot for a cup of tea (Esther brought along some delicious homemade strudel), they began to compare cosmopolitan Rome with provincial Melbourne. In Rome they used to go to the opera. Every café engaged five singers to entertain the customers. As Esther described Rome, fluent Italian phrases appeared in her speech. If Italy and the Braws hadn't been so destitute and war-torn, they would never have parted company. One could say they became passive in Rome, or one could say they were simply enjoying a well-deserved respite.

But they moved on to new adventures and a new "normal life" in Melbourne and then to Jerusalem. Somehow, Shmuel learned to survive and to adapt and enjoy life by being helpful to others and sharing his stories. He became a typical Jew, extraordinary in many ways.

Chapter Eleven

A Poem about Tarnow

Many people have lived through experiences similar to Shmuel's, and even worse. Accounts that describe the horrors inflicted by the Nazis and the Soviets are not scarce. Over a million Jewish children were killed during the Holocaust. One of them was Shmuel's ten-year-old daughter. Knowing that makes our hearts ache, but our hearts ached already.

Our personal interest in Shmuel was, of course, a Jewish interest, but his human qualities are not uniquely Jewish. Shmuel always had non-Jewish friends, both in Poland and in Australia. He was an attractive, affable man, warm, open, honest, and deeply concerned for other people. One winter evening Calvin drove him home, just a few blocks from the study in Talpiot, where we spent many evenings reviewing and recording his life, listening to his stories and learning about his past. As he was getting out of the car, he noticed a neighbor of his, an elderly woman, entering a taxicab. "Oh, oh," he said, "Something's wrong. I think her husband must be sick." Shmuel stood in the cold for quite a while, staring after the cab, worried about his neighbor. He was not someone who avoided people's problems or shirked responsibility for helping friends or neighbors.

He is not the least bit bitter about what happened to him. Angry? Yes. Shocked at the injustice? Yes. Sad? Yes. But not bitter. He did not become a misanthropist. We once complimented him on his good nature. He shrugged our words off, but conceded that he was driven neither by hatred nor envy, "*nisht sinna, nisht kinna.*" I like people." After decades of disappointments, tragedies, betrayals, and loss, Shmuel's heart remained on his sleeve. He liked people and was vulnerable emotionally.

Shmuel's stories often told us the unexpected, providing insights about life in Poland and about human nature in general. We found ourselves repeating them to our friends, and telling them about Shmuel himself. The more we heard from Shmuel, the more attached the three of us grew to each other, and the more the interviews meant to all of us. We began discussing possible uses of the material with friends, soliciting their reactions. The most common one was, "I know someone you should talk to." Israel swarmed with fascinating old people. Everybody had a story: the Austrian gent with flowing whiskers who was a journalist in Spain during the Civil War; the Kurdish owner of an automobile body shop who had driven armored vehicles to besieged Jerusalem under fire from the Arab Legion; the sweet pediatrician who was born in Moscow and spoke Russian, French, and Hebrew at home, studied medicine at the Sorbonne in the twenties, and then moved to Palestine; the Yugoslavian smelter who fought with the partisans, was sent to Auschwitz, survived, and saved the life of the orphaned daughter of the collaborator who had delivered him to the Gestapo; and thousands of others. One met them at every turning, and most of them would have loved to pass their stories on.

Shmuel used to tell his family and friends that he was spending one evening a week "talking to the professor," proud of the attention we were paying him.

"What does he have to say to you so much?" Esther, his wife, once asked us.

By sitting with Shmuel and giving him a chance to remember what he had lived through and to tell it, we created an event whose reverberations were felt beyond the walls of the book-lined study where it was taking place. The interviews affected all three of us, our families, and our friends.

Among the friends who took a deep interest in our project was Harold Schimmel, a Hebrew poet and translator of Hebrew to English. Harold attended the synagogue with Shmuel, sat in the row in front of him, so he was acquainted with our subject. Harold was a devoted reader of Yiddish poetry, and when Shmuel first appeared in the neighborhood, he had entertained a fantasy that he was a Yiddish writer. Shmuel had that air about him. When you heard him speak Yiddish and saw the animated expression on his face, you could tell why one might have taken him for a poet or retired actor.

We were sorry to disabuse Harold, but his disappointment was not long-lived. When he heard about the life that Shmuel had actually lived, his curiosity was aroused. We wanted to invite him one evening, but we were reluctant to disrupt the intimate atmosphere of trust that had grown in our sessions. Fortunately, an occasion emerged that made it perfectly natural to invite Harold. In his research on Yiddish poetry Harold came upon a poet from Galicia who lived and wrote in the United States, Reuben Iceland, (also known as Ruben Eisland) among the founders of the modernistic school of Yiddish writing, *Di Yunge*. One of Iceland's best known poems written in 1919 is called "Tarnow." We showed it to Shmuel, who was enthralled. We asked him whether he would be willing to read it to Harold in his native Galician accent, and Shmuel agreed with pleasure.

The following week Harold joined us, and Shmuel recited the poem, commenting on it as he went along. The poem is not an easy one. It is not very long but is written in a modernistic idiom. Here and there Shmuel stumbled on words, unusual coinages of the poet and his circle, but he read it with grace, poise and dramatic effect. He let the poem's rhythm guide his voice, which became more resonant as he recited and he appreciated what he was reading. Even though the poem was written in New York when Shmuel was a young man, by a poet who had left Galicia before Shmuel was born, he agreed that it was the same place, his Tarnow.

The poem evokes the wonderful smells of Tarnow's market and daily life and also the pogroms of the past; the serenity of the Sabbath, the special foods eaten on Friday night, and the warmth and beauty of family life.

Tarnow

A poem by Reuben Iceland (1884-1955) born in Radomysl Wielki

(near Tarnow), the first of three stanzas:

> It smells of saffron, cloves and herbs,
> Sweet gingerbread and sharp kummel,
> Odors of cloth, and rust and iron,
> And with the cold of long bars of steel,
> It smells of sacks and rotting straw,
> Baskets and boxes and trunks that tell
> Of distant towns and foreigners,
> And more than anything from that particular town,
> To me the dearest in the whole wide world
> My loveliest childhood dream—Tarnow

> You are not so big, nor particularly beautiful,
> You, the best loved of my towns.

You lie pressed between two mountains,
Like a huge bird, with two long spread wings,
One right, one left.
But you are big
With the proud tread of your merchants,
Large with the noise of thousands
Who come to trade within your gates,
And bigger still with your life-giving breath,
That spreads along the roads,
And animates forty towns and hundreds of villages all
round

And you are beautiful among your daughters,
The loveliest of Galicia's lovely daughters.
And you are beautiful with the blue shimmer
Over your red roofs.
Yet loveliest of all,
With your green fires, that light up in rows,
In the eyes of a young boy
Who catches a glimpse of you from the mountain.
Even lovelier and bigger in the shiver of my childhood
dreams.

The third stanza of the poem ends with:

And more than anything about that particular town,
For me it was the dearest in the wide world
It was my loveliest childhood dream—
Tarnow

From time to time, Shmuel would stop reading, look up, and say, "That's right. That's just how it is."

During our final formal session, after hearing him recite the poem, we asked him what he thought we were doing, why we were interviewing him.

"Do you have any idea what we're going to do with this stuff?"

"I'm not one hundred percent sure what's going on. I don't know what you want to do. You want to write something? Sure."

"It's a lot of interesting material."

"It's a lot of nonsense, too."

"We've tried to cut out the nonsense and stick to what we think is important. We want to see if everybody else agrees that you're a fascinating person."

"It's not a big deal, from my side, whether it is printed, and it's not a big loss."

"We think it is a big deal."

"Mine feeling, what I thought, is not what I'm telling you. Sometimes it's very painful, and sometimes it's getting..." Shmuel paused, looking for a word, "it's getting emotional. You're comparing it in your mind, and it hits you. That is not what you expect."

We try to explain to him that many of us are from the same place, a place like Tarnow. Here our point of view differs profoundly with his. He is only willing to generalize as far as Polish Jewry. "The Jewish life in Poland was everywhere mostly the same." Shmuel is careful to point out the difference between big cities, such as Krakow, where the Jews were mostly business people, and Tarnow, where they were workers. Tarnow is too real and immediate for Shmuel to see it as "the town from which we all come" in one disguise or another. We feel that way even though we are not ourselves of Galician stock, and sometimes Shmuel's stories of the outlandish behavior of the Hasidim remind us of just what our own grandparents might have warned us against. However, Shmuel's Tarnow still strikes us as the place from which twentieth century Jewry springs, a closed largely traditional Jewish society set in a hostile environment, opening towards the West, full of turbulent energy, and helpless against the violent forces that were to overwhelm it. For us it is "Anywhere" in Eastern Europe. For Shmuel it is "mine Tarnow."

One of the enigmas about Israeli society for anyone trying to cope with it is the apparent eclipse of many traditional Jewish traits. Jews were meek and deferential to non-Jews. Israelis are arrogant and disdainful to the rest of the world. Jews were physical cowards; Israelis are tough soldiers. Jews were warm, effusive, emotionally demonstrative people. Israelis are restrained and taciturn. Shmuel wanted very much to find Tarnow again when he moved to Israel, so to him Israel simply didn't feel Jewish enough. His disappointment with Israel was one of the recurrent themes of our conversations. We tried to sharpen the paradox for Shmuel by asking him how he could explain what had happened. "How did Israeli society get to be the way it is, if everyone came from a place like Tarnow, the Tarnows of the world?"

Perhaps that was an unfair question. We were asking Shmuel to acknowledge that Tarnow was not as idyllic as he remembered. For all the spontaneous charity he recalls, some Jews exploited their brethren mercilessly in Eastern Europe. Not everyone was God-fearing and content with his lot. Millions of Jews fled from places like Tarnow, partially because of their poverty, partially because of persecution and pogroms, and also partially to free themselves from the narrow confines of an oppressive social system. The only thing that kept the Polish Jews in place during the perilous, economically depressed years before World War II was the impossibility of finding a place of refuge. Israel was founded by people who had rejected Tarnow categorically, Tarnow and a thousand other towns and cities where Jews suffered almost as much from their benighted coreligionists as from their hostile gentile neighbors. In his own lifestyle, as he implicitly told us, Shmuel too had rejected traditional Tarnow. He was never an integral part of his father's world of bearded Jews in long black coats. However, Shmuel could not admit that there were aspects of Tarnow that he did not miss. To make such an admission would be to retrospectively lend a hand to the Nazis

Shmuel simply took our challenging question very literally. He explained that only a small percentage of Israelis are Polish Jews. The Russian immigrants, for example, have been cut-off from *Yiddishkeit* (Jewishness) for two or three generations. That explains why Israel is so little like Tarnow, of blessed memory.

Shmuel misses the brotherhood he remembers from his youth, living among people who all spoke Yiddish with the same accent. Almost everyone in Israel who was born in the Diaspora has similar longings, if not for the Yiddish of Tarnow, then for the Judaeo-Persian of Teheran (rather than that of Meshhad or Isfahan). Everyone living in Israel thinks that Israel is less closely knit than the Jewish society of their nostalgic memories, whether in the Diaspora or in Palestine before the establishment of the State. No consistent attitude toward the traditional Jewish past has yet been worked out in modern Israel. Thoughtful people among the children of those who tried to create a completely new social order have come to see that they need to re-establish contact with the past, but they do not yet know upon what terms. Where do we fit in Jewish history? And where does Jewish history fit into our lives?

The struggle of Israeli culture with Jewish history is made more immediate by the presence within Israeli society of Jews who seem to live in the past. The streets teem with black-coated Jews harking back to Eastern Europe as well as old men and women from Yemen and North Africa who have not forsaken traditional dress. Moreover, there are throngs of survivors like Shmuel. Once, when Jeff was waiting for a bus in the Tel Aviv area, talking with a friend in English about Shmuel's experiences in Siberia, a man in front of him turned around and said in Yiddish-accented English, "That's my story!" He proceeded to tell how he and his family had been sent from the Ukraine to Siberia, where he had worked in lumber camps. After they got on the bus he continued talking, moving on to kabalistic esoterica concerning the approaching end of days. On another occasion, we met a young navy officer named Pedro and asked him how he got such an uncommon name. "I was born in Portugal." We asked, "Are you descended from the ancient Portuguese Jewish community?" "No, my parents are Polish Jews." His mother's family reached Lisbon in the early years of the twentieth century, stayed and prospered. His father was sent from Poland to Siberia during the war, released from a labor camp weighing some thirty-five kilos, and drafted into Andersarmee (Ander's Army). He deserted in Palestine, where he met his future wife, a volunteer nurse for the Haganah. With us when we met Pedro was an Israeli in his thirties who was born in Poland of parents who had had similar experiences. The father of a close friend of ours, an extremely French Parisienne, was a textile worker in Lodz before the war. He fled to Uzbekistan from the ghetto, and there he built looms out of surplus railroad ties and established a black market textile industry. After the war he went into business in France, and years later his daughter moved to Israel.

Although few of the Jews of Poland and the rest of Eastern Europe survived the war, a great number of those who did, and their children, are alive and busy in modern Israel. Shmuel's story is partially theirs, as it is partially that of every Jew in the modern world. But the next generation has fewer connections to the world of their grandparents and fewer insights in the daily life of ordinary Jews like Shmuel.

The psychological stress undergone by survivors is a subject well-investigated today. Naturally we asked Shmuel about his feelings as a survivor, about the effects of his ordeal, and about the lessons he might have drawn from it. What wisdom could he pass on to those who were fortunate enough not to suffer what he did? His reactions to those questions brought out his human qualities to the fullest.

We constantly marveled at how normal Shmuel seemed, as if he had overcome his past. When we told him that, he agreed with us. He said he had made a great effort to free himself from the burdens of his tragic memories. "I talk things over to mine self, not out loud. I talk to mine self. I say to mine self, you got to live a normal life, a normal life. What you got to *shlepp* that baggage with you? When I had the children, and I start playing with them, the feeling of being a *mensh* is coming back. You have to put it out of your mind. You can't live with that all the time in your mind. You get cuckoo. It's finished. Maybe you get to be a criminal, or you can kill somebody. Also I tell that advice to other people, and that is helping me."

Shmuel never tried to make us feel sorry for him. He did not feel sorry for himself. His sympathies were with those who suffered and died. Rather than pity himself, Shmuel tried to help other people. "What can you do? *Shrei gevalt* (cry out)? You have to face it. It's finished. I don't even know where they are. I know where my mother is, and my sisters and brothers-in-law. But the others? I don't know. What can I do? Open the grave? Where is lying 25,000 people? I put the memorial stone in the wall. Maybe it's there, maybe it's not. I don't know. You can't trust the Poles. The show is going on. Life is a show. I was sorry for years. I'm sorry now, but time heals. You cool down. Even now the Jewish people have a philosophy. You don't say Kaddish (the mourner's prayer) twenty years. You observe *Yortsait* (a yearly date of death) once a year."

Shmuel had said that for a long time after the war he never went to synagogue, and it was only upon Esther's insistence that he took it up again. We wanted to know whether the war had made Shmuel anti-religious. "Not anti-religious, just empty." Then, leaning forward, in low, confidential tones, Shmuel told us what he never would admit publicly to anyone: "Just between us, for a long time, *davening* and *shul*, even God don't mean a thing to me, till now!" He sat back, and then he continued. "Why do I have to thank the *Ribono Shel Olom* (the Master of the universe) that He let be killed six million Jews?"

"But He saved you"

Shmuel was very upset "*A groisse vergnug*! (big deal!). Two and a half million Polish Jews killed like dogs. Thank you very much. Why special me?"

"Do you feel guilty because you survived?"

"Think of the Rebbes who were killed, the Szabner. And I am a little nothing. The explanation was not mine. Some religious people got anti-religious. I lived a normal life for thirty-five years. Then for four or five years, the war. After that I am leading a double life. It is not that I am wearing Polish clothes and clothes from here. But in my mind I'm leading a double life. I told you I get crazy. I get ideas that I'm afraid to say. I ask myself questions, I told you, a lot of questions. There is no answer. About Jewish things. Then it is very hard. I would never have that ideas in Poland."

Individuals like Shmuel survived, and their faith was shaken. But the Jewish people survived as well, stricken gravely, but still able to stage a recovery. We asked Shmuel whether he thought it was valuable for the Jewish people as a whole to survive as a people.

"It's a very hard question," he acknowledged. "I was thinking a lot about that question. What is the big deal about being a Jew? Is that a *metziah* (bargain)? To be always for thousands and thousands of years the *kapporah* (scapegoat) for someone? Can't we mix together with everybody, so forget about it? *Vus iz di hochma*? (What's the big deal?) Give me an answer. *Vus iz di hochma*?"

But Shmuel did not wait for our answer. He told us an anecdote about a Jew who was sitting peaceably by himself. Christian missionaries came to harangue him. The Jew listened and listened, agreeing with many of their arguments against Judaism, but he would not be convinced to convert. Finally, the missionaries lost their patience. "Why won't you convert, Jew?" The Jew calmly answered, "Why do I have to change my shit for your shit? Is the other one better?" He used the same expression when he was telling us about his life in Australia.

"That is my answer," Shmuel told us. "You got no option. Why do I have to change it? It's not worse than the other one. In a way it's even better. I'm not a nationalist. I'm not even a Zionist. After the war I come to a conclusion that all, socialism, liberalism, *herut-menshen* (right-wing Zionism), is not worth even *di shubn fun a tsibl* (an onion peel): Nothing. It's just play. You are a Jew. What kind of color you put on, that's not important."

"You could avoid a lot of suffering if you stopped being Jewish," we suggest provocatively to Shmuel.

"How are other nations better?"

"They're not being persecuted."

"You can't stop being a Jew. My grandchildren are Jews, and their grandchildren will be Jews. I want to be a Jew."

"Do you believe in God?"

"You asked me a question I wanted to ask you."

"I asked first. You don't have to answer."

"It's no harm. Listen, if I make another sin, what's the difference? If you got a thousand, you got a thousand and one. It's a fifty-fifty feeling, sometimes yes, sometimes no. Times have changed. Everybody has a God. The Chinese and the Indians and the Arabs. So only the Jews have a real god? After the war you see something else, but before the war I never think like that."

Despite the religious doubts awakened in him by the war, Shmuel acknowledged the need to remember, to pass the knowledge of his experiences on.

"Will you tell your grandson?"

"Of course. If I'm still alive, I'll tell him."

"Is it important to tell him?"

"In a way, yes I will tell you why. It is not a reminder just for ourselves, because we are old people. We can do nothing.

"We have to remind our children, because it's our existence. People are ninety-five percent against us, and maybe it's coming again. You got to be on your feet. Don't forget it. To the young people it's very important, that they know. Like here, to remind them that the PLO has killed six people from the *shul*."

Shmuel was referring to the murders in Hebron in the spring of 1980. "Don't talk about whether they got a right to go there. That they could *daven* in Kiryat Arba (a religious settlement near Hebron). But the fact, innocent people was killed in the street on their way back from *shul*. If you forget, the Jewish people is lost forever, slowly, but lost."

In another mood, however, Shmuel denied that his experience could teach anything. "It's useless, because younger people haven't felt what we felt. You know that someone is hurt, that he is suffering. But you don't feel what he is feeling, even if you feel sorry."

"In other words, there's no message to give?"

"No. No. I wonder, how could God allow that to happen to His people? When my kids ask me that question, I can't answer it. I told you I got a split... I am still half the normal life in Poland, no questions about anything. Sometimes when I was a boy, I give my father a question, he says, 'too much questions,' and I stop. I still ask questions. It drives me cuckoo sometimes. I'm not the only one. You got thousands who are still alive. They ask questions." Knowing that others have survived what he lived through brought Shmuel no spiritual comfort.

In the end, Shmuel's painful memories cut him off from the rest of humanity. He discussed his return to Tarnow again.

"I was dreaming of that minute to come back to that little town. When I left Tarnow everything was there, the buildings, the houses, except people was not living in four rooms, but in one room. The streets the same, everything the same. But when you come back, half a city is wiped out. You don't know where you go. I see a friend of mine. He is sitting on a stone, crying like a little child. And I started crying too. A half a city just doesn't exist. You don't know what that feeling is."

"No, but you do, and you can tell us."

Everyone who reaches the age of seventy-four lives with vivid images of people who have died long ago, of a world that has been swallowed up by change and modernization, if not by war and Holocaust. Shmuel told us, "I am a man in the last phase from the life." Without any special sense of bitterness, he said that he could no longer keep up with change:

"Maybe time is moving too fast for me now."

Older people commonly dwell on memories of the distant past, and Shmuel certainly knew that. Yet he was surprised when it happened to him. "You know, I am still living half in that life." He told us how he sometimes sat down and drifted into a daydream without being aware of it, losing himself in recollections of Tarnow. Then he had to rouse himself. "I'm not home. I'm in Israel and that's forty years back. I remember a lunch, a party, you know. It's coming to me."

We told him we had an unfair question: "Are you afraid of death?" Shmuel answered with no hesitation.

"No, because I am no longer young."

It distressed him to see his faculties deteriorate. "Every day you sink slowly. What kind of life is that?" When he was younger, he could get up at four in the morning with no special effort. Now he liked to sleep late. He felt himself slowing down. He never wore long underwear in his life, but now he did. The cold got to him. He also feared loneliness. If, God forbid, he were left alone, he knew he would neglect himself, not cook any food. He had clearly thought the subject through.

On what was Shmuel's Judaism based then? He was not sure whether he believed in God. The afterlife was of little speculative interest to him; the thought of it brought him no comfort.

"Why did you go to *shul* today, and keep kosher?" We ask him. Again he had a ready answer:

"First thing, don't forget, up until 1939, the first thirty-three years of my life, I was one hundred percent in Jewish life. I like very much that thirty-three years of my life. When I come to *shul*, next to me sits this one, that one. That feeling, a warm feeling. That's why I keep coming to *shul*. I got a friend. He is always asking why some things are not allowed on Shabbat. I never asked. I keep Shabbat, because the Jewish people have always kept Shabbat. *Menshen habens gemacht. Vi soll ich nisht machen?*" (People have always done it. How could I not do it?).

In Tarnow, long ago, a Jew named Blonsky returned from America with a little money and opened a shop in the Christian neighborhood. Blonsky decided to stay open on Shabbat, the only Jewish shop in Tarnow to do so. How did the Jewish community react? "One *Shabbos* a few people put on *talesim* (prayer shawls) and the cap, and they go down to Blonsky to remind him it was *Shabbos*. Not just make trouble. They said, '*Gut Shabbes, gut Shabbos*,' and he shut the shop." That is the world to which Shmuel is still loyal.

During the war Shmuel's older brother Ze'ev joined the Polish army in exile. Ze'ev was a tall, strapping, blond man who spoke perfect Polish. The other soldiers, Catholics, advised him to claim that he was Catholic too, but Ze'ev would not. He allowed the army officials to ignore his Jewishness, but he never represented that he was anything other than what he was. Similarly with Shmuel: after he was released from the Siberian camp, a Catholic Polish man connected with the army in exile told Shmuel he would get a better job and be taken from the USSR if he didn't mention his Jewishness on the official questionnaire. "I told him, 'I was all my life a Jew, and you made me a good Jew.' I refused to sign that." Such religious commitment and loyalty defies rational explanation, and we asked Shmuel for none.

Sometimes Shmuel felt depressed: he could see no future for Judaism. The war uprooted the plant and poisoned its native soil.

So where are we supposed to get our *yiddishkeit*? If Tarnow and places like Tarnow contained the only authentic Judaism, and they are all destroyed, then what about the people born after the destruction? Where can they find real

Jewishness? Shmuel was hard hit by the question. "I don't have an answer." From his point of view, Judaism today was without foundations.

We asked the question in a different way: "How can your daughter Rivka manage to live a full Jewish life? Where does she draw her Judaism?"

"She agrees with me," Shmuel answered. "She got it from her parents."

"So won't her children get it from her?"

Shmuel was not sure. He saw Judaism getting weaker and weaker as time went on. But we refused to let up. We remembered Shmuel's telling us that his three year old grandson already knew the *Modeh Ani*, the first morning prayer: "I am grateful to You, O living and eternal Sovereign, for restoring my soul to me in compassion. Great is Your faithfulness."

"Don't you feel terrific and satisfied when you hear your grandson say the *Modeh Ani*, Shmuel?"

"Yes," he admitted, "I do."

Epilogue

Kibbutz Ein Zurim, Israel
July 2008

We drove from Jerusalem to Ein Zurim (by way of B'nei Brak, a city that reminded us of the Poland of our nineteenth century imagination) to reconnect with Rivka, Shmuel's daughter, and to visit Esther, Shmuel's widow. Esther was sixteen years younger than Shmuel, only twenty-five when they met and married in Tarnow on their way to Italy. She had survived the devastation in her town in the Ukraine and lost her whole family who lived there. She was now eighty-six years old. Shmuel passed away in 1992, sixteen years earlier.

We spent a good part of the late afternoon reviewing our trip a few weeks earlier to Tarnow and hearing the details about Rivka's subsequent visit to Lvov and Kreminetz. We looked at the pictures that Rivka had taken of Tarnow and heard of the reactions of Rivka's children to our visit to their grandfather's birthplace. We spoke briefly to Esther who is no longer very mobile and largely confined to her home in this Kibbutz. She has powerful and vivid memories of Shmuel and his last weeks, when he no longer was Shmuel. As always Esther shared with us her joy in Rivka's children and her grandchildren.

Then Rivka, my wife Fran and I went to the cemetery where Shmuel is buried, a rural spot not far from Kibbutz Ein Zurim. There is no greenery in this cemetery, only concrete walkways, stones and silence, quiet and peaceful. In a stark, arid space with a strong white background, made even sharper by the blinding setting sun, Shmuel Braw found his final resting place. I couldn't help thinking about the contrast between the cemetery in Tarnow and the one near Ein Zurim. Shmuel the son of Reb Meir from Tarnow, buried in Israel, finally at rest alongside others from other places and times. A space in front of his grave is reserved for his beloved Esther.

His date of birth is listed as the 13th of Sivan (June 6th) 1906 and the date of death as the 11th of Iyar (May 14th) 1992. A short verse from the Psalms was inscribed on the stone at the foot of the grave. It was suggested by a Yemenite member of Kibbutz Ein Zurim who had not known Shmuel, but it seemed to us, especially to Rivka, that he had selected a most fitting verse for her father. The verse was from Psalm 85 verse 11:

Kindness and truth have met;
justice and peace have kissed.

As is the custom, we left a small stone on top of Shmuel's grave to remind us and notify Shmuel that we had been there. Yehe Zichro Baruch. May his memory be a blessing.

About the Authors

Calvin Goldscheider

Calvin Goldscheider is Professor Emeritus of Sociology and Ungerleider Professor Emeritus of Judaic Studies at Brown University. He completed his undergraduate degree at Yeshiva University and his PhD at Brown University. He was Professor of Sociology and Demography at the Hebrew University of Jerusalem, Israel having taught there from 1969-1985. He has held faculty appointments at the University of Southern California, the University of California, Berkeley, Brandeis University as well as Stockholm University, Sweden. He is now affiliated with American University, Washington, DC and its Center for Israel Studies. His major research publications have focused on the sociology and demography of ethnic populations, historically and comparatively, with an emphasis on family and immigration. He is the author. co-author, or editor of 25 books including *The Transformation of the Jews; Jewish Continuity and Change; Israel's Changing Society; The Arab-Israeli Conflict;* and *Studying the Jewish Future.* He has also published over 150 articles in peer-reviewed social science journals and edited collections. He has received a number of honors including the Sklare Award for his distinguished career by the Association of Jewish Studies and held a Fulbright in Sweden.

Jeffrey M. Green

Jeffrey M. Green came to Israel in 1973 with his wife and daughter. He earned a BA from Princeton and a PhD in Comparative Literature from Harvard. After teaching for a few years at the Hebrew University, Jerusalem, he became a free-lance translator and writer. His translations include several novels by the eminent Hebrew writer, Aharon Appelfeld. His books include *A Daughter's Gift of Love* by Trudi Birger with Jeffrey Green, a Holocaust memoir that has appeared in more than a dozen languages including German, Japanese, Spanish, Finnish, Hebrew, and Dutch and reissued in paperback by the Jewish Publication Society. He has also written *Thinking Through Translation*, published by the University of Georgia Press and two books in Hebrew. He has recently published *Largest Island in the Sea.*